African Adventures

Teacher's Guide

Unit 3

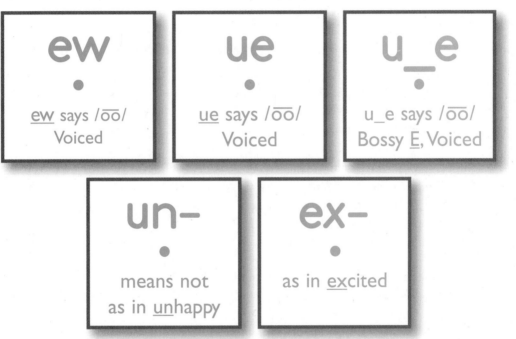

ew · <u>ew</u> says /o͞o/ Voiced	ue · <u>ue</u> says /o͞o/ Voiced	u_e · u_e says /o͞o/ Bossy <u>E</u>, Voiced
un– · means not as in <u>un</u>happy	ex– · as in <u>ex</u>cited	

Note: See New and Important Objectives on page 2 for a complete list of skills taught and reviewed.

Critical Foundations in Primary Reading

Marilyn Sprick, Ann Watanabe, Karen Akiyama-Paik, and Shelley V. Jones

Cambium LEARNING® Group

Voyager LEARNING

ISBN 13-digit: 978-1-60218-526-5
ISBN 10-digit: 1-60218-526-3

8 9 10 11 12   B&B   17 16 15 14 13

166861/9-13

Table of Contents
Unit 3
African Adventures

How to Teach the Lessons

Letter Sounds and Combinations

Cumulative Review of *Read Well 1* Sounds and Combinations (Ss, Ee, ee, Mm, Aa, Dd, th, Nn, Tt, Ww, Ii, Th, Hh, Cc, Rr, ea, sh, Sh, Kk, -ck, oo, ar, wh, Wh, ĕ, -y as in fly, Ll, Oo, Bb, all, Gg, Ff, Uu, er, oo as in book, Yy, a schwa, Pp, ay, Vv, Qq, Jj, Xx, or, Zz, a_e, -y as in baby, i_e, ou, ow as in cow, ch, Ch, ai, igh, o_e, ir) and:

Unit 2	Unit 3			Unit 5	Unit 6
aw	**ew**	**ue**	**u_e**	**ow**	**ge**
/aw/	/o͞o/	/o͞o/	/o͞o/	/ō͞ō/	/j/
P<u>aw</u>	**Cr<u>ew</u>**	**Bl<u>ue</u>**	**Fl<u>u</u>t<u>e</u>**	**Sn<u>ow</u>**	**Pa<u>ge</u>**
Voiced	Voiced	Voiced	Bossy <u>E</u> Voiced	Voiced (Long)	Voiced

Unit 6	Unit 7		Unit 8		Unit 10
-dge	**ci**	**ce**	**kn**	**ph**	**oa**
/j/	/sss/	/sss/	/nnn/	/fff/	/ō͞ō/
Ba<u>dge</u>	**<u>Ci</u>rcle**	**<u>Ce</u>nter**	**<u>Kn</u>ee**	**<u>Ph</u>one**	**B<u>oa</u>t**
Voiced	Unvoiced	Unvoiced	Voiced	Unvoiced	Voiced (Long)

Unit 11		Unit 12		Unit 13	
oi	**ea**	**gi**	**au**	**oy**	
/oi/	/ĕĕĕ/	/j/	/au/	/oy/	
P<u>oi</u>nt	**Br<u>ea</u>d**	**<u>Gi</u>raffe**	**Astron<u>au</u>t**	**B<u>oy</u>**	
Voiced	Voiced (Short)	Voiced	Voiced	Voiced	

Affixes (including morphographs—affixes taught with meaning) and Open Syllables

Cumulative Review of *Read Well 1* Affixes (-ed, -en, -es, -ing, -ly, -s, -y, -tion) and:

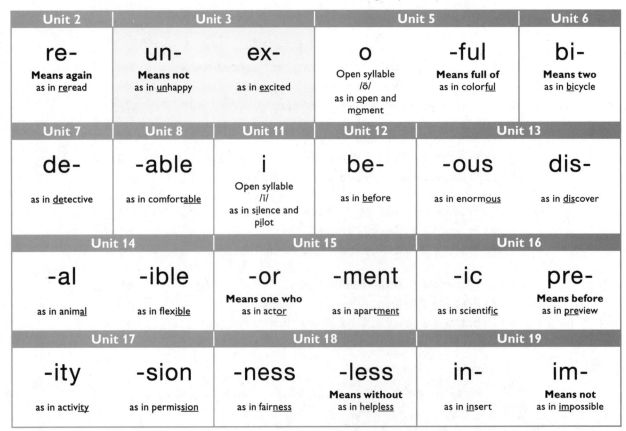

Unit 2	Unit 3		Unit 5		Unit 6
re-	**un-**	**ex-**	**o**	**-ful**	**bi-**
Means again	**Means not**		Open syllable	**Means full of**	**Means two**
as in <u>re</u>read	as in <u>un</u>happy	as in <u>ex</u>cited	/ō/	as in color<u>ful</u>	as in <u>bi</u>cycle
			as in <u>o</u>pen and m<u>o</u>ment		

Unit 7	Unit 8	Unit 11	Unit 12	Unit 13	
de-	**-able**	**i**	**be-**	**-ous**	**dis-**
as in <u>de</u>tective	as in comfort<u>able</u>	Open syllable /ī/ as in s<u>i</u>lence and p<u>i</u>lot	as in <u>be</u>fore	as in enorm<u>ous</u>	as in <u>dis</u>cover

Unit 14		Unit 15		Unit 16	
-al	**-ible**	**-or**	**-ment**	**-ic**	**pre-**
		Means one who			**Means before**
as in anim<u>al</u>	as in flex<u>ible</u>	as in act<u>or</u>	as in apart<u>ment</u>	as in scientif<u>ic</u>	as in <u>pre</u>view

Unit 17		Unit 18		Unit 19	
-ity	**-sion**	**-ness**	**-less**	**in-**	**im-**
			Means without		**Means not**
as in activ<u>ity</u>	as in permis<u>sion</u>	as in fair<u>ness</u>	as in help<u>less</u>	as in <u>in</u>sert	as in <u>im</u>possible

Introduction
African Adventures

Story Notes

Miss Tam in Africa: The newly retired Miss Tam is off on her first travel adventure—a grand trip to Ghana. In Ghana, Miss Tam begins a series of experiences that celebrate both the diversity and shared customs of people around the world. Wherever Miss Tam goes, she will eat rice, buy shoes, find storytellers, and make new friends.

The River Horse: Start with a riddle. A few clues might help. Two of its teeth can grow to 20 inches long. It can't swim, but spends all day in the water. What's behind the curtain? The endangered African hippo is a fascinating subject that captivates young readers.

> **CAUTION**
> **(Reminder)**
> Do not read the Read Aloud recommendations during small group instruction. Reserve this time for students to read.

Recommended Read Alouds

The *Read Well 2* suggested Read Alouds enhance small group instruction—providing opportunities to further build background knowledge and vocabulary.

Owen and Mzee by Isabella Hatkoff, Craig Hatkoff, Paula Kahumbu, and Peter Greste
Nonfiction • Narrative

In December 2004, a devastating tsunami separated a young hippo from his family. Rescued and sent to an animal preserve in Kenya, the frightened hippo formed a remarkable friendship with a 130-year-old giant tortoise named Mzee. The book chronicles their touching relationship.

Read Well Connections
Through *Owen and Mzee*, students learn more facts about hippos and the wildlife of Africa. The book also reinforces lessons learned in earlier units about forming friendships despite differences. In future *Read Well 2* units, students will read more about Miss Tam and tsunamis.

NOTE FROM THE AUTHORS

> **ASSISTING ENGLISH LANGUAGE LEARNERS AND CHILDREN WITH LANGUAGE DELAYS**
> Throughout the day, use *Read Well* vocabulary words in informal conversation. For example, you may wish to review the word "habit" as students are washing their hands. Say something like:
> [Jose], what are you doing?
> If the student does not respond, gently prompt:
> [Jose], say "I am washing my hands." (I am washing my hands.)
> Yes, you are washing your hands. Washing your hands is a good *habit*!

New and Important Objectives
A Research-Based Reading Program

Phonemic Awareness
Phonics
Fluency
Vocabulary
Comprehension

Phonological and Phonemic Awareness

Isolating Beginning, Middle, and Ending Sounds; Segmenting; Blending; Rhyming; Onset and Rime; Counting Syllables

Phonics

Cumulative Letter Sounds and Combinations

Review • Ss, Ee, ee, Mm, Aa, Dd, th, Nn, Tt, Ww, Ii, Th, Hh, Cc, Rr, ea, sh, Sh, Kk, -ck, oo, ar, wh, Wh, ĕ, -y (as in fly), Ll, Oo, Bb, all, Gg, Ff, Uu, er, oo (as in book), Yy, a (schwa), Pp, ay, Vv, Qq, Jj, Xx, or, Zz, a_e, -y (as in baby), i_e, ou, ow (as in cow), ch, Ch, ai, igh, o_e, ir, aw

Cumulative Affixes and Morphographs

Review • -ed, -en, -er, -es, -est, -ing, -ly, -s, -y, -tion, re-

★New Letter Sounds, Combinations, Affixes, Morphographs, and Related Words

ew (as in crew) • crew, drew, flew, grew, stew

ue (as in blue) • blue, clue, glue

u_e (as in flute) • dune, flute, June, Luke, mule, prune, rule, rude, tube, tune

un- • undo, unfolded, unkind, unlock, unlocked

ex- • exact, excite, exciting, explain

★New Abbreviations

AL, St., USA

★New Contractions

won't

★New Proper Nouns

African, Akwaaba, Anansi, Ghana, Kwesi, Kwesi's, Minnie Bird, Miss Tam's, Montgomery, Mr. Moffitt, Puddle, Scraggly Cat, Western

---

∗ **Known Pattern Words With Affixes, Known Tricky Words With Affixes,** and **Known Multisyllabic Words With Affixes** have base words students have previously read. The words are new in this unit because they have not been previously read with the affix.

★ = New in this unit

Phonics (continued)

★ New Pattern Words

bank, banked, bean, beans, bold, both, cheat, craft, crafts, graze, guide, held, hire, hired, horse, horses, inches, lean, meats, palm, press, print, printed, ray, rink, robe, screech, screeched, shake, shaking, size, skirt, spoke, stall, stared, stiff, tale, taped, tear, tire, tired, tore, van, wade, waded, wait, waiting, wake, wider

*Known Pattern Words With Affixes • breathes, brightly, closed, crawled, driving, faster, filled, hardly, hopes, hunting, liked, meats, mostly, mouths, noses, parting, played, pouted, reached, refill, rider, skating, sleeping, spends, thanked, tried, wider, yawned

★ New Compound and Hyphenated Words

airport, bittersweet, breakfast, footwear, goodbye, hatpin, postcards, someone's, storyteller, storytellers, wildlife

★ Other New Multisyllabic Words

adult, agreed, arrive, arrived, baby, baskets, bottom, during, evening, habit, hippo, hippopotamus, hippos, hippo's, impress, insult, later, manners, monkey, monkeys, peppers, protect, protected, retired, return, sandal, sandals, sturdy, toddle, toddled, tomatoes, trickster, whispered, window

*Known Multisyllabic Words With Affixes • drummers, lessons, perfectly, respectfully

★ New Tricky Words

balance, balanced, bargain, bargained, beautiful, bowl, curtain, dangerous, daughter, elephants, finally, fruit, full, grow, half, herbivore, herbivores, honest, hotel, hour, hours, library, love, onions, rĕ̄ad, rice, shoe, shoes, southern, spider, though, village, weigh, weighs, worry

*Known Tricky Words With Affixes • carrying, colors, eyes, friendly, walking, world's

Fluency

Accuracy, Expression, Phrasing, Rate

Vocabulary

New • adventure, Africa, amazing, bargain, custom, Ghana, graze, habitat, herbivore, insult, manners, protected, respectfully, sturdy, trickster, wildlife

Review • bittersweet, continent, habit, hesitate, neighborhood, ordinary, respect

Reviewed in Context • amazed, bittersweet, continent, habit, hesitate, ordinary, popular, pout, respect, vast

Idioms and Expressions

Reviewed in Context • bird's-eye view

Comprehension

Unit Genres

Nonfiction • Expository
Fiction • Realistic Narrative, Imaginative Narrative

Comprehension Processes

Build Knowledge: Factual, Procedural, Conceptual

Day	1	2	3	4	5	6
Remember						
Defining						
Identifying (recalling)	S,C	S,C	S,C	S,C	E,S	S,C
Using		S	S			
Understand						
Defining (in your own words)			C			S
Describing		S	S		S,C	S
Explaining (rephrasing)	S	S	S	S	S,C	S
Illustrating						
Sequencing					C	
Summarizing				S	S,C	S
Using	S,C	S,C	S,C	S,C	S,C	S,C
Visualizing						
Apply						
Demonstrating	S	S				
Explaining (unstated)		S	S		E,S	S,C
Illustrating		C	C	C		
Inferring	S,C	S	S	S,C	S	S,C
Making Connections (relating)	S		S		S	
Predicting	S		S	S	S	S
Using	S	S	S	S,C	S	S
Analyze						
Classifying		C		C		
Comparing/Contrasting				S		
Distinguishing Cause/Effect						
Drawing Conclusions					E	C
Inferring					S	S
Evaluate						
Making Judgments					S	C
Responding (personal)					S	
Create						
Generating Ideas						C

E = Exercise, S = Storybook, C = Comprehension & Skill

Comprehension (continued)

Skills and Strategies

Day	1	2	3	4	5	6
Priming Background Knowledge	S		S			S
Setting a Purpose for Reading						
Answering Questions	S	S	S	S	S	S
Asking Questions						
Visualizing		C	C	C		
Comprehension Monitoring/Fix Ups						
Does it Make Sense?	C	C	C		C	C
Looking Back				C		C
Restating						
Summarizing						
Main Idea						
Retelling						
Supporting Details						
Understanding Text Structure						
Title, Author, Illustrator	S	S		S		S
Fact or Fiction						
Genre (Classifying)						
Narrative						
Setting			S	S	S,C	
Main Character/Traits (Characterization)	S	S,C	C	S	C	
Goal	S	S		S	C	
Problem/Solution						
Action/Events/Sequence		C		S	S	
Outcome/Conclusion					C	
Lesson/Author's Message					S	
Expository						
Subject/Topic						C
Heading						S,C
Supporting Details (Facts/Information)					E	S,C
Main Idea		C		C		
Using Graphic Organizers						
Chart						
Diagram (labeling)						
Hierarchy (topic/detail)						
K-W-L						
Map (locating, labeling)						
Matrix (compare/contrast)						
Sequence (linear, cycle, cause and effect)						
Story Map					C	
Web					C	

E = Exercise, S = Storybook, C = Comprehension & Skill

Comprehension (continued)

Study Skills

Day	1	2	3	4	5	6
Alphabetical Order			C			
Following Directions	C					
Locating Information		S			E	S,C
Note Taking						
Previewing						S
Reviewing		S	S	S	S	S
Test Taking						
Using Glossary						
Using Table of Contents	S					S
Viewing						
Verifying						

Writing in Response to Reading

Day	1	2	3	4	5	6
Sentence Completion		C	C	C	C	C
Making Lists						C
Sentence Writing		C	C	C		C
Story Retell/Summary					C	
Fact Summary					E	C
Paragraph Writing						
Report Writing						
Open-Ended Response						C
Creative Writing						

Writing Traits

(Addressed within the context of Writing in Response to Reading)

Day	1	2	3	4	5	6
Ideas and Content						
Elaborating/Generating						
Organization						
Introduction						
Topic Sentence						
Supporting Details						
Sequencing					C	
Word Choice						
Sophisticated Words (Tier 2 and 3)						
Conventions						
Capital		C	C	C	C	C
Ending Punctuation	C	C	C	C	C	C
Other (commas, quotation marks)						
Presentation						
Handwriting						
Neatness						

E = Exercise, S = Storybook, C = Comprehension & Skill

Daily Lesson Planning

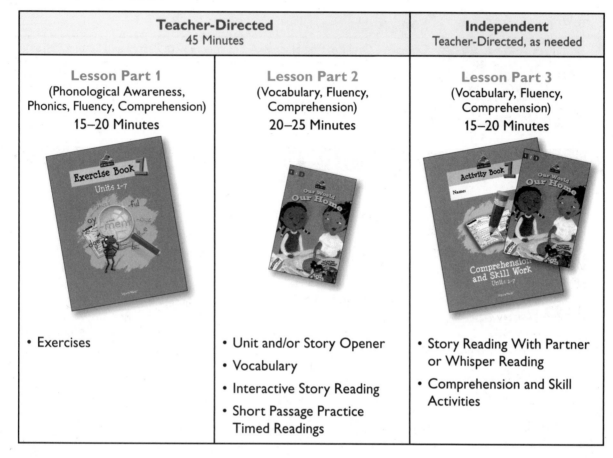

Teacher-Directed 45 Minutes		Independent Teacher-Directed, as needed
Lesson Part 1 (Phonological Awareness, Phonics, Fluency, Comprehension) 15–20 Minutes	**Lesson Part 2** (Vocabulary, Fluency, Comprehension) 20–25 Minutes	**Lesson Part 3** (Vocabulary, Fluency, Comprehension) 15–20 Minutes
• Exercises	• Unit and/or Story Opener • Vocabulary • Interactive Story Reading • Short Passage Practice Timed Readings	• Story Reading With Partner or Whisper Reading • Comprehension and Skill Activities

HOMEWORK

Read Well Homework (blackline masters of new *Read Well 2* passages) provides an opportunity for children to celebrate accomplishments with parents. Homework should be sent home on routine days.

ORAL READING FLUENCY ASSESSMENT

Upon completion of this unit, assess each student and proceed to Unit 4, as appropriate. See Making Decisions at the end of the unit for additional information.

DIFFERENTIATED LESSON PLANS

The differentiated lesson plans illustrate how materials can be used for students with various learning needs. As you set up your unit plan, include *Read Well 2* Exercises and Story Reading on a daily basis. Unit 3 includes 6-, 8-, 9-, 10-, and 11-Day Plans.

Plans	For groups that:
6-DAY	Complete Oral Reading Fluency Assessments with Passes and Strong Passes
8-DAY	Complete Oral Reading Fluency Assessments with Passes and require teacher-guided assistance with Story Reading and Comprehension and Skill Work
9-, 10-, or 11-DAY	Have difficulty passing the unit Oral Reading Fluency Assessments

6-DAY PLAN

Day 1	Day 2	Day 3
Teacher-Directed • Exercise 1 • Unit and Story Opener: African Adventures, Miss Tam in Africa • Vocabulary, Ch. 1, 2 • Miss Tam in Africa, Ch. 1 • Guide practice, as needed, on Comp & Skill 1a, 1b, 2 **Independent Work** • Repeated Reading: Whisper Read, Miss Tam in Africa, Ch. 1 • Comp & Skill 1a, 1b, 2 **Homework** • Homework Passage 1	**Teacher-Directed** • Exercise 2a • Exercise 2b: Focus Lesson • Miss Tam in Africa, Ch. 2 • Guide practice, as needed, on Comp & Skill 3, 4 **Independent Work** • Repeated Reading: Partner or Whisper Read, Miss Tam in Africa, Ch. 2 • Comp & Skill 3, 4 **Homework** • Homework Passage 2	**Teacher-Directed** • Exercise 3 • Vocabulary, Ch. 3, 4 • Miss Tam in Africa, Ch. 3 • Guide practice, as needed, on Comp & Skill 5, 6 **Independent Work** • Repeated Reading: Partner or Whisper Read, Miss Tam in Africa, Ch. 3 • Comp & Skill 5, 6 **Homework** • Homework Passage 3
Day 4	**Day 5**	**Day 6**
Teacher-Directed • Exercise 4 • Miss Tam in Africa, Ch. 4 • Guide practice, as needed, on Comp & Skill 7, 8 **Independent Work** • Repeated Reading: Partner or Whisper Read, Miss Tam in Africa, Ch. 4 • Comp & Skill 7, 8 **Homework** • Homework Passage 4	**Teacher-Directed** • Exercise 5 • Vocabulary, Ch. 5 • Miss Tam in Africa, Ch. 5 • Guide practice, as needed, on Comp & Skill 9, 10 **Independent Work** • Repeated Reading: Partner or Whisper Read, Miss Tam in Africa, Ch. 5 • Comp & Skill 9, 10 **Homework** • Homework Passage 5	**Teacher-Directed** • Exercise 6 • Vocabulary • Story Opener: The River Horse • The River Horse • Guide practice, as needed, on Comp & Skill 11, 12 **Independent Work** • Repeated Reading: Partner or Whisper Read, The River Horse • Comp & Skill 11, 12 • Oral Reading Fluency Assessment **Homework** • Homework Passage 6

Note: Unit 3 features an extra Just for Fun Comp & Skill activity, located after Activity 12. This page can be used any time during this unit or taken home for fun.

8-DAY PLAN • *Pre-Intervention*

Day 1

Teacher-Directed
- Exercise 1
- Unit and Story Opener: African Adventures, Miss Tam in Africa
- Vocabulary, Ch. 1, 2
- Miss Tam in Africa, Ch. 1
- Guide practice, as needed, on Comp & Skill 1, 2

Independent Work
- Repeated Reading: Whisper Read, Miss Tam in Africa, Ch. 1
- Comp & Skill 1, 2

Homework
- Homework Passage 1

Day 2

Teacher-Directed
- Exercise 2a
- Exercise 2b: Focus Lesson
- Miss Tam in Africa, Ch. 2
- Guide practice, as needed, on Comp & Skill 3, 4

Independent Work
- Repeated Reading: Partner or Whisper Read, Miss Tam in Africa, Ch. 2
- Comp & Skill 3, 4

Homework
- Homework Passage 2

Day 3

Teacher-Directed
- Exercise 3
- Vocabulary, Ch. 3, 4
- Miss Tam in Africa, Ch. 3
- Guide practice, as needed, on Comp & Skill 5, 6

Independent Work
- Repeated Reading: Partner or Whisper Read, Miss Tam in Africa, Ch. 3
- Comp & Skill 5, 6

Homework
- Homework Passage 3

Day 4

Teacher-Directed
- Exercise 4
- Miss Tam in Africa, Ch. 4
- Guide practice, as needed, on Comp & Skill 7, 8

Independent Work
- Repeated Reading: Partner or Whisper Read, Miss Tam in Africa, Ch. 4
- Comp & Skill 7, 8

Homework
- Homework Passage 4

Day 5

Teacher-Directed
- Exercise 5
- Vocabulary, Ch. 5
- Miss Tam in Africa, Ch. 5
- Guide practice, as needed, on Comp & Skill 9, 10

Independent Work
- Repeated Reading: Partner or Whisper Read, Miss Tam in Africa, Ch. 5
- Comp & Skill 9, 10

Homework
- Homework Passage 5

Day 6

Review
- Miss Tam in Africa, selected chapters

Teacher-Directed
- Exercise 3
- Miss Tam in Africa, selected chapters
- Check and correct Comp & Skill 1–10 (selected tasks)

Independent Work
- Repeated Reading: Partner or Whisper Read, Miss Tam in Africa, selected chapters
- Correct and complete Comp & Skill 1–10

Homework
- Comp & Skill 2 (Passage Fluency)

Day 7

Teacher-Directed
- Exercise 6
- Vocabulary
- Story Opener: The River Horse
- The River Horse

Independent Work
- Repeated Reading: Partner or Whisper Read, The River Horse
- Comp & Skill 11, 12
- Oral Reading Fluency Assessment

Homework
- Homework Passage 6

Day 8

Review
- The River Horse

Teacher-Directed
- Exercise 5
- The River Horse
- Correct and complete Comp & Skill 11, 12 and guide practice on Just for Fun

Independent Work
- Repeated Reading: Partner or Whisper Read, The River Horse
- Correct and complete Comp & Skill 11, 12, and Just for Fun

Homework
- Comp & Skill 8 (Passage Fluency)

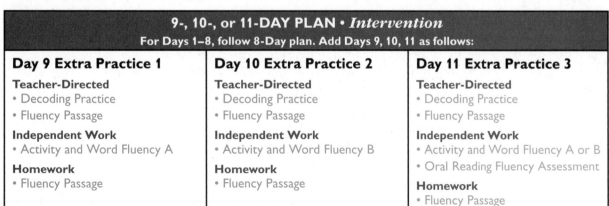

9-, 10-, or 11-DAY PLAN • *Intervention*
For Days 1–8, follow 8-Day plan. Add Days 9, 10, 11 as follows:

Day 9 Extra Practice 1

Teacher-Directed
- Decoding Practice
- Fluency Passage

Independent Work
- Activity and Word Fluency A

Homework
- Fluency Passage

Day 10 Extra Practice 2

Teacher-Directed
- Decoding Practice
- Fluency Passage

Independent Work
- Activity and Word Fluency B

Homework
- Fluency Passage

Day 11 Extra Practice 3

Teacher-Directed
- Decoding Practice
- Fluency Passage

Independent Work
- Activity and Word Fluency A or B
- Oral Reading Fluency Assessment

Homework
- Fluency Passage

Materials and Materials Preparation

Core Lessons

Teacher Materials

READ WELL 2 MATERIALS
- Unit 3 Teacher's Guide
- Sound Cards
- Unit 3 Oral Reading Fluency Assessment found on page 86
- Group Assessment Record found in the *Assessment Manual*
- Miss Tam's World Map

SCHOOL SUPPLIES

Stopwatch or watch with a second hand

Student Materials

READ WELL 2 MATERIALS (for each student)
- *Our World, Our Home* storybook
- World map copies (located on the CD)
- *Exercise Book 1*
- *Activity Book 1* or copies of Unit 3 Comprehension and Skill Work
- Unit 3 Certificate of Achievement/Goal Setting (BLM, page 87)
- Unit 3 Homework (blackline masters)
  See *Getting Started* for suggested homework routines.

SCHOOL SUPPLIES

Pencils, colors (optional—markers, crayons, or colored pencils)

> Make one copy per student of each blackline master, as appropriate for the group.
>
> *Note:* For new or difficult Comprehension and Skill Activities, make overhead transparencies from the blackline masters. Use the transparencies to demonstrate and guide practice.

> **FOCUS LESSONS**
> For Exercises 2b and 5b (Focus Lessons), make overhead transparencies from the blackline masters, write on transparencies placed over the pages, or use paper copies to demonstrate how to complete the lessons.

Extra Practice Lessons

> **CAUTION**
> Use these lessons only if needed. Students who need Extra Practice may benefit from one, two, or three lessons.

Student Materials

READ WELL 2 MATERIALS (for each student, as needed)

See Extra Practice blackline masters located on the CD.
- Unit 3 Extra Practice 1: Decoding Practice, Fluency Passage, Word Fluency A, and Activity
- Unit 3 Extra Practice 2: Decoding Practice, Fluency Passage, Word Fluency B, and Activity
- Unit 3 Extra Practice 3: Decoding Practice, Fluency Passage, Word Fluency A or B, and Activity

SCHOOL SUPPLIES

Pencils, colors (markers, crayons, or colored pencils), highlighters

Acknowledging Accomplishments

Some children are internally motivated to learn new skills. Other children need your guidance and support. All students are motivated by your enthusiasm! Use words, privileges, personal records, and notes to keep children excited about their accomplishments. Be creative.

CELEBRATE ACCOMPLISHMENTS— WHETHER BIG OR SMALL

When students meet your expectations, acknowledge individuals and provide descriptive feedback.

- [Rashad], thank you for waiting for your turn.
- [Ella], I could see you whisper reading while [Josh] read. Excellent.

Provide attention with privileges.

- [Luisa], you kept your place, so you get the next turn.
- [Tyrell], you waited for your turn, so you get to help me be the teacher. Come on up and help me point to the words on the board.

Use physical demonstrations.

- Everyone, thumbs up for [Alejandro]. He just used a snazzy word. What word did he just use? (ordinary)
- Everyone, air clap for [Kate]. She read each word carefully.

Write notes home that congratulate students and family members. Acknowledgments are motivating.

- Write notes to family members thanking them for their participation.
- Give kids sticky notes to acknowledge their accomplishments.
  [Angie], you get a sticky note with the word *habitat*. You used that snazzy word in your answer. Good thinking.

Have students keep records of their personal bests.

- Provide each student with a Personal Best Scrapbook.
  At the end of each unit, have students review their work and add their favorite written work to the scrapbook.
- Provide each student with a plastic sleeve.
  At the end of each unit, have students review their work and place a new piece of their best written work in the plastic sleeve.
- Place each child's personal best oral reading fluency score on a sticky note in his or her reading folder. Replace, as appropriate.

SAMPLE PARENT NOTE

Dear Mr. Jefferson,

Rashad improved his oral reading fluency by 5 words correct per minute this week. Congratulations to Rashad and you. Reading at home makes a difference. Thanks so much for your help.

Sincerely,
Mr. Bird

---

habitat

herbivore

What to Do When Comprehension Breaks Down

Gray text questions help students build a cohesive understanding of the story. The questions also direct students to information that will help them make inferences.

PROCEDURES

If students have difficulty comprehending:
- think aloud with them and/or
- reread the portion of the story that answers the question,
- then repeat the question.

For example, in Story Reading 6 of this unit, students try to figure out what's behind a curtain. What could be as big as one small car but weigh as much as two cars? After solving the riddle, students read a brief paragraph about hippos. Then they are asked two gray text questions.

The first question is literal.
What does hippopotamus mean?
If students can't answer, direct them back to the text. Say something like:

Think aloud, then guide rereading of the text.

I can't remember either.
I do remember the book told us what that big word means.
What can we do to find the answer? (reread)
Yes, that's what good readers do.
Everyone, reread the first sentence.
(Hippopotamus is a big word that means river horse.)
The book told us "Hippopotamus is a big word that means . . . (river horse).

Restate the question.

What does hippopotamus mean?
(river horse)

WITH THE TEACHER

What animal is this?

The amazing hippopotamus!

A Hippo's Size

Hippopotamus is a big word that means river horse. Hippos are much bigger than horses though. They are only four to five feet tall, but they can weigh more than your family's car!

What does *hippopotamus* mean? Why is that a good name?

86

The second question is inferential. Why is that a good name?
The answer builds on background knowledge. If the students can't answer, think aloud with them and guide their responses. Help students make connections with their background knowledge.

Think aloud, then help students use their background knowledge to make an inference.

Why is *river horse* a good name? Let's close our eyes and imagine a big horse. Now imagine a hippo standing next to it. Does a hippopotamus look a little like a horse? (Yes, but it is bigger.)
Yes, a hippo has four legs, two ears that stand up, and a muzzle-like nose.
So it looks a little like a horse. What does hippopotamus mean? (river horse)

Where do you think hippos live? (in rivers)
Nod your head if you think *river horse* is a good name.
Why do you think so? (It's an animal that looks a little like a horse and it lives in rivers.)

How to Teach the Lessons

Teach from this section. Each instructional component is outlined in an easy-to-teach format.

Exercise 1

- Unit and Story Opener: African Adventures, Miss Tam in Africa
- Vocabulary
- Story Reading 1
  With the Teacher: Chapter 1
- Comprehension and Skill Activities 1, 2

Exercise 2a

- Exercise 2b: Focus Lesson
- Story Reading 2
  With the Teacher: Chapter 2
- Comprehension and Skill Activities 3, 4

Exercise 3

- Vocabulary
- Story Reading 3
  With the Teacher: Chapter 3
- Comprehension and Skill Activities 5, 6

Exercise 4

- Story Reading 4
  With the Teacher: Chapter 4
- Comprehension and Skill Activities 7, 8

Exercise 5a

- Execise 5b: Focus Lesson
- Vocabulary
- Story Reading 5
  With the Teacher: Chapter 5
- Comprehension and Skill Activities 9, 10

Exercise 6

- Vocabulary
- Story Opener: The River Horse
- Story Reading 6
  With the Teacher: The River Horse
- Comprehension and Skill Activities 11, 12

Note: Lessons include daily homework.

① SOUND REVIEW
Use selected Sound Cards from Units 1 and 2.

PACING
Exercise 1 should take about 15 minutes.

★② NEW SOUND INTRODUCTION
- Tell students <u>e-w</u> says /o͞o/ as in crew, and <u>u-e</u> says /o͞o/ as in blue.
- Have students look at the picture, identify "crew" and "blue," and read the sentence.
  The *crew* works on the *new blue* ship.
- Have students practice: <u>e-w</u> says /o͞o/ as in crew, <u>u-e</u> says /o͞o/ as in blue.
- Have students read the sentence again, then identify the words with /o͞o/ as in crew and /o͞o/ as in blue.
- For Rows B and C, have students read the underlined sound, then the word.
- Have students go back and read the whole words. Provide repeated practice.

③ ACCURACY AND FLUENCY BUILDING
A2. Rhyming Words

Have students read each set of words. Ask students how each set of words is the same.

B1. Bossy <u>E</u>
- Have students identify how the words are the same.
- Have students identify the underlined sound and then read the word.

C2, D1. Multisyllabic Words

For each word, have students read and finger count each syllable, then read the word. Use the word in a sentence, as appropriate.

E2. Tricky Words
- For each Tricky Word, have students identify known sounds or word parts. Use the word in a sentence to help with pronunciation.
- If the word is unfamiliar, tell students the word.

breakfast
Look at the first word. The first part is a little tricky; it says /brĕk/.
Read the word by parts with me. break-fast
George likes ham and eggs for . . . *breakfast.*
Read the word three times. (breakfast, breakfast, breakfast)

adventure	Miss Tam wanted to go on an . . . *adventure.*
eye	I can close one . . . *eye.*
been	Where have you . . . *been?*

ACCURACY AND FLUENCY BUILDING (Reminder)
- For each task, have students say any underlined part, then read the word.
- Set a pace. Then have students read the whole words in each task and column.
- Provide repeated practice, building accuracy first, then fluency.

④ MORPHOGRAPHS
- Remind students that a morphograph is a word part that means something.
- ★Introduce "un = not."
  Look at Row A. The morphograph *un-* means not. So we can say that *un-* equals not.
  Everyone, read that with me. *Un-* equals not.

- For each word, have students read what the word means and the accompanying sentence. Have students rephrase the sentence.
  Un- means not, so unhappy means not happy. Unhappy equals not happy.

Everyone, read that with me. Unhappy equals not happy. Now read the sentence. (She is unhappy when she is sick.) That means . . . she is not happy when she is sick.

• Repeat with "unkind equals not kind."

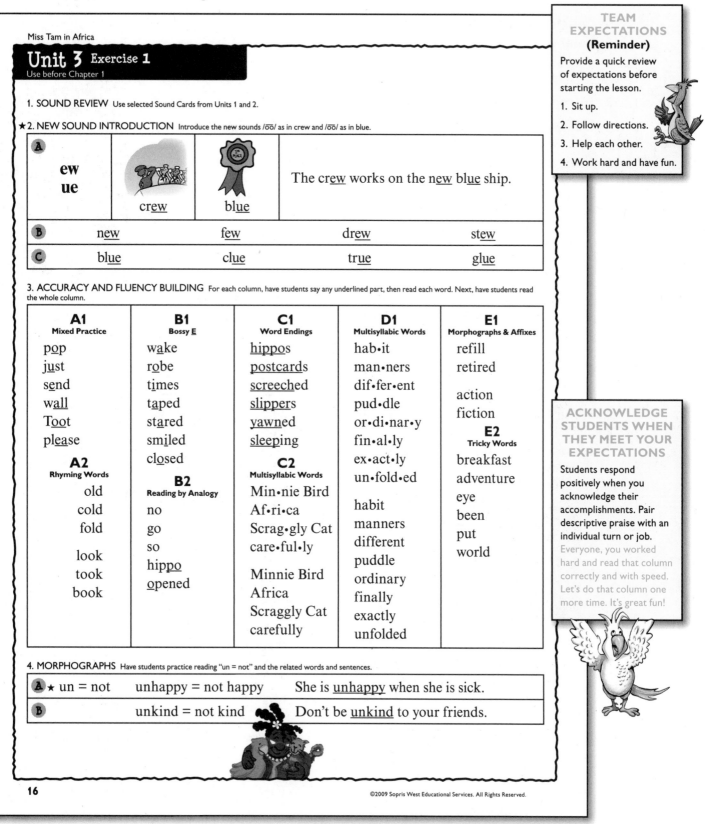

TEAM EXPECTATIONS (Reminder)

Provide a quick review of expectations before starting the lesson.

1. Sit up.

2. Follow directions.

3. Help each other.

4. Work hard and have fun.

Miss Tam in Africa

Unit 3 Exercise 1
Use before Chapter 1

1. SOUND REVIEW Use selected Sound Cards from Units 1 and 2.

★2. NEW SOUND INTRODUCTION Introduce the new sounds /o͞o/ as in crew and /o͞o/ as in blue.

A	ew ue	crew	blue	The cr<u>ew</u> works on the n<u>ew</u> bl<u>ue</u> ship.
B	n<u>ew</u>	f<u>ew</u>	dr<u>ew</u>	st<u>ew</u>
C	bl<u>ue</u>	cl<u>ue</u>	tr<u>ue</u>	gl<u>ue</u>

3. ACCURACY AND FLUENCY BUILDING For each column, have students say any underlined part, then read each word. Next, have students read the whole column.

A1 Mixed Practice	B1 Bossy E	C1 Word Endings	D1 Multisyllabic Words	E1 Morphographs & Affixes
p<u>o</u>p	w<u>a</u>ke	<u>hippo</u>s	hab·it	refill
just	r<u>o</u>be	<u>postcard</u>s	man·ners	retired
send	t<u>i</u>mes	<u>screech</u>ed	dif·fer·ent	
w<u>a</u>ll	t<u>a</u>ped	<u>slipper</u>s	pud·dle	action
T<u>oo</u>t	st<u>a</u>red	<u>yawn</u>ed	or·di·nar·y	fiction
please	sm<u>i</u>led	<u>sleep</u>ing	fin·al·ly	E2 Tricky Words
A2 Rhyming Words	cl<u>o</u>sed	C2 Multisyllabic Words	ex·act·ly	breakfast
old	B2 Reading by Analogy	Min·nie Bird	un·fold·ed	adventure
cold	no	Af·ri·ca		eye
fold	go	Scrag·gly Cat	habit	been
	so	care·ful·ly	manners	put
look	<u>hippo</u>		different	world
took	<u>opened</u>	Minnie Bird	puddle	
book		Africa	ordinary	
		Scraggly Cat	finally	
		carefully	exactly	
			unfolded	

4. MORPHOGRAPHS Have students practice reading "un = not" and the related words and sentences.

A ★	un = not	unhappy = not happy	She is <u>unhappy</u> when she is sick.
B		unkind = not kind	Don't be <u>unkind</u> to your friends.

ACKNOWLEDGE STUDENTS WHEN THEY MEET YOUR EXPECTATIONS

Students respond positively when you acknowledge their accomplishments. Pair descriptive praise with an individual turn or job. Everyone, you worked hard and read that column correctly and with speed. Let's do that column one more time. It's great fun!

PREPARATION

Have Miss Tam's world map and/or student copies of the map ready to use as a reference.

COMPREHENSION PROCESSES

Remember, Understand, Apply

PROCEDURES

1. **Introducing the Unit and Story**

   Identifying—Title; Inferring; Priming Background Knowledge; Using Table of Contents; Predicting

   • Tell students the title of their new unit is "African Adventures."

   Today, we're going to start a new unit called "African Adventures." What's the title of the unit? (African Adventures)

   The stories in this unit take place in one setting.

   Where do you think that is? (Africa)

   What do you already know about Africa? (It's a place faraway. Africa has lions . . .)

   Everyone, turn to page 5. This is the Table of Contents for the unit. Find the title of the first story we're going to read. What's the title? (Miss Tam in Africa)

   What do you think is going to happen in this story?

   • Think aloud with students. Summarize their comments. Say things like:

   [Carlos] thinks Miss Tam is going to go to Africa. He said that he could tell that by the title.

   • Using Miss Tam's map, show students where you live, where Miss Tam lives in Montgomery, and Ghana. If students have their own maps, have them touch each place and label Ghana. Discuss briefly how Miss Tam will get to Ghana.

TABLE OF CONTENTS

UNIT 3 • **African Adventures**

5

UNIT 3
African Adventures

58

Miss Tam in Africa
by Jessica Sprick
illustrated by Paige Eastburn O'Rourke

Who is this story about?¹ Where does the story take place?² Find Miss Tam.³
What do you think she will do in this story?⁴

59

• Have students look at the picture on the title page and answer the gray text questions.

COMPREHENDING
AS YOU GO

❶ **Remember:** Identifying—Main Character (The story is about Miss Tam.)
❷ **Apply:** Inferring (in a park, in Africa . . .)
❸ **Remember:** Identifying—Main Character
❹ **Apply:** Predicting (She will go on a trip, travel, see new things . . .)

COMPREHENSION PROCESSES

Understand, Apply

PROCEDURES

Introducing Vocabulary

> ☆ manners ☆ Africa
> ☆ adventure ☆ sturdy
> ☆ Ghana

- For each vocabulary word, have students read the word by parts, then read the whole word.
- Read the student-friendly explanations to students as they follow with their fingers. Then have students use the vocabulary word by following the gray text.
- Review and discuss the photos and illustrations, as appropriate.

> **USING VOCABULARY**

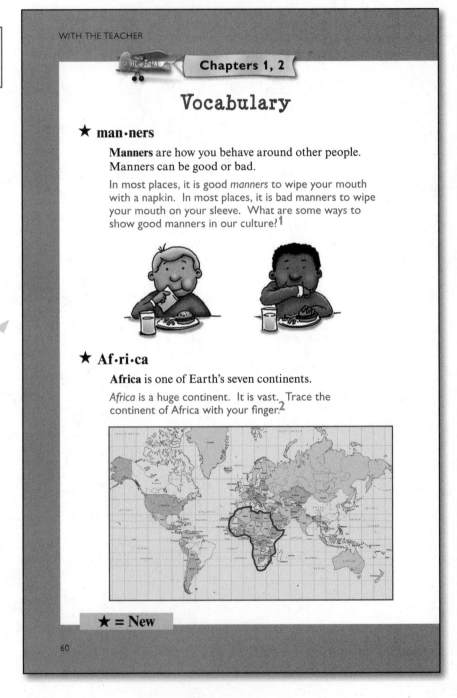

WITH THE TEACHER

Chapters 1, 2

Vocabulary

★ **man·ners**

Manners are how you behave around other people. Manners can be good or bad.

In most places, it is good *manners* to wipe your mouth with a napkin. In most places, it is bad manners to wipe your mouth on your sleeve. What are some ways to show good manners in our culture?[1]

★ **Af·ri·ca**

Africa is one of Earth's seven continents.

Africa is a huge continent. It is vast. Trace the continent of Africa with your finger.[2]

★ = New

60

❶ Apply: Making Connections; Using Vocabulary—manners (Saying "please" and "thank you" are ways to show good manners. Chewing with your mouth closed is good manners . . .)

❷ Apply: Demonstrating; Using Vocabulary—Africa

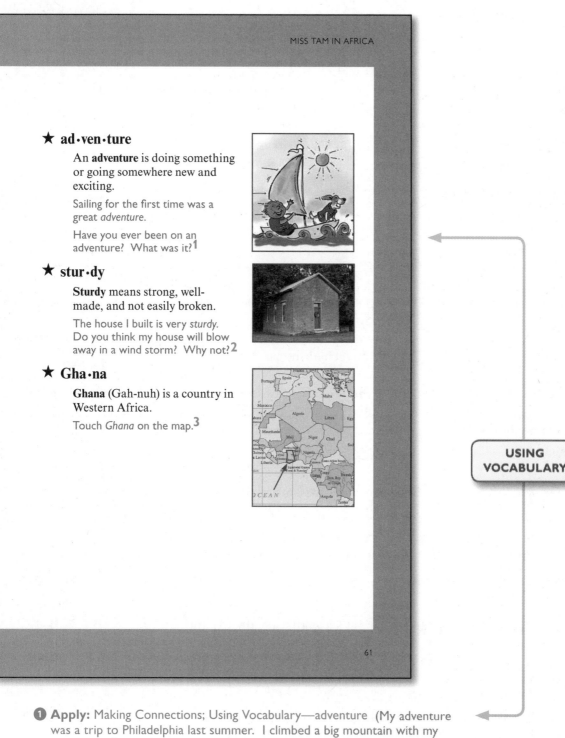

MISS TAM IN AFRICA

★ **ad·ven·ture**

An **adventure** is doing something or going somewhere new and exciting.

Sailing for the first time was a great *adventure*.

Have you ever been on an adventure? What was it?[1]

★ **stur·dy**

Sturdy means strong, well-made, and not easily broken.

The house I built is very *sturdy*. Do you think my house will blow away in a wind storm? Why not?[2]

★ **Gha·na**

Ghana (Gah-nuh) is a country in Western Africa.

Touch *Ghana* on the map.[3]

61

USING VOCABULARY

❶ **Apply:** Making Connections; Using Vocabulary—adventure (My adventure was a trip to Philadelphia last summer. I climbed a big mountain with my cousins . . .)

❷ **Understand:** Inferring; Explaining; Using Vocabulary—sturdy (No, your house is sturdy.)

❸ **Apply:** Demonstrating; Using Vocabulary—Ghana

CHAPTER 1 INSTRUCTIONS
Students read with the teacher.

COMPREHENSION PROCESSES
Remember, Understand, Apply

COMPREHENSION BUILDING
- Encourage students to answer questions with complete sentences.
- If students have difficulty comprehending, think aloud with them or reread the portion of the story that answers the question. Repeat the question.

PROCEDURES

1. Introducing Chapter 1

Identifying—Title; Predicting

Have students read the title and predict what will happen in Chapter 1.

2. First Reading
- Ask questions and discuss the story as indicated by the gray text.
- Mix group and individual turns, independent of your voice. Have students work toward a group accuracy goal of 0–3 errors. Quietly keep track of errors made by all students in the group.
- After reading the story, practice any difficult words. Reread the story if students have not reached the accuracy goal.

3. Second Reading, Short Passage Practice: Developing Prosody
- Demonstrate expressive, fluent reading of the first paragraph. Read at a rate slightly faster than the students' rate. Say something like:
  Listen to me read the first two paragraphs. I'm going to emphasize words that are important.

  "At *exactly* 6:30 a.m., Minnie Bird *screeched*, 'Good morning!'

  It had been Miss Tam's habit for *30 years* to pop out of bed, put on her slippers, and put on her robe. However, this morning was *different*. It was not an ordinary day. Miss Tam was *not* going to . . ."

- Guide practice with your voice.
  Read the paragraph with me.

- Provide individual turns while others track with their fingers and whisper read.
- Repeat with one paragraph at a time. Repeat steps with each remaining paragraph.

4. Whisper Reading: Repeated Reading
Have students finger track and whisper read before beginning independent work.

5. Homework 1: Repeated Reading

> **CORRECTING DECODING ERRORS**
> During story reading, gently correct any error, then have students reread the sentence.

> **REPEATED READINGS**
> **Prosody**
> On the second reading, students practice developing prosody—phrasing and expression. Research has shown that prosody is related to both fluency and comprehension.

COMPREHENDING AS YOU GO

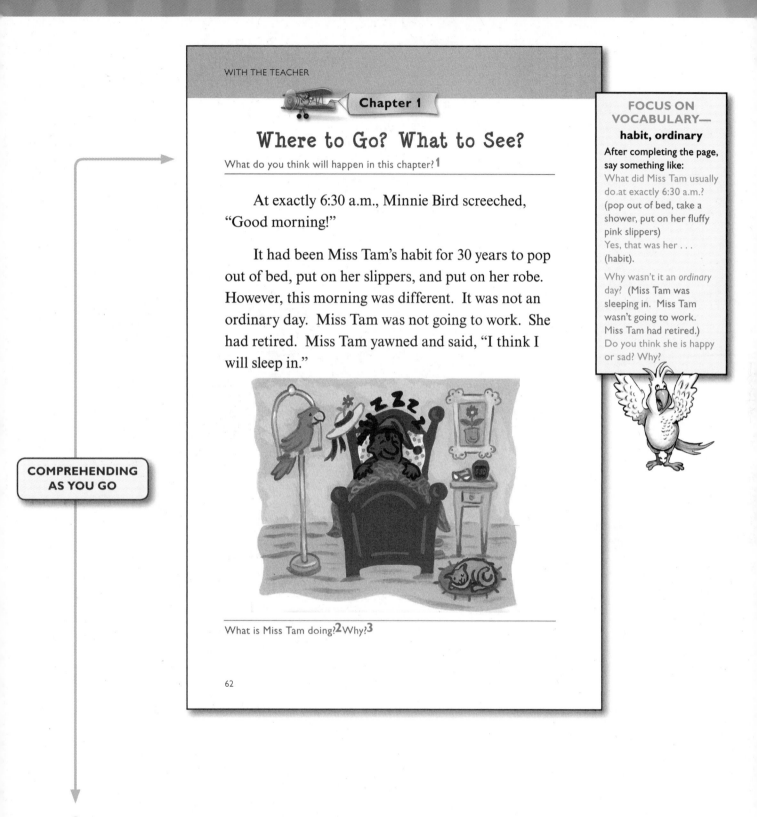

WITH THE TEACHER

Chapter 1

Where to Go? What to See?

What do you think will happen in this chapter? **1**

At exactly 6:30 a.m., Minnie Bird screeched, "Good morning!"

It had been Miss Tam's habit for 30 years to pop out of bed, put on her slippers, and put on her robe. However, this morning was different. It was not an ordinary day. Miss Tam was not going to work. She had retired. Miss Tam yawned and said, "I think I will sleep in."

What is Miss Tam doing? **2** Why? **3**

62

❶ **Apply:** Predicting (Miss Tam will go somewhere. She will find out where to go and what to see . . .)

❷ **Remember:** Identifying—What (Miss Tam is sleeping in.)

❸ **Apply:** Inferring (She is retired, so she doesn't have to get up and go to work.)

MISS TAM IN AFRICA

As was his habit, Old Scraggly Cat opened one eye and closed it again.

Finally, at exactly 7:00 a.m., Minnie Bird screeched, "Please, wake up! Seeds, please."

No, it was not an ordinary day. Miss Tam was sleeping late. Miss Tam opened one eye and smiled. "Minnie Bird, what good manners you have."

After breakfast, Miss Tam took out *Toot and Puddle* and 10 books about Africa.

"It's time to plan my first grand adventure," said Miss Tam.

Why does Miss Tam think Minnie Bird has good *manners?*¹ Why isn't it an ordinary day?² Look at the picture. What is Miss Tam doing?³

63

COMPREHENDING
AS YOU GO

❶ **Apply:** Inferring; Using Vocabulary—manners (Minnie Bird has good manners because she says "please.")

❷ **Understand:** Explaining; Using Vocabulary—ordinary (It's not an ordinary day because Miss Tam is sleeping in.)

❸ **Understand:** Explaining; Using Vocabulary—adventure (Miss Tam is looking at books about Africa. Miss Tam is planning her first grand adventure.)

WITH THE TEACHER

Miss Tam carefully unfolded a world map and taped it to the wall.

"Bird's-eye view. Bird's-eye view," screeched Minnie Bird.

Miss Tam stared at the world map for a long time. "I will go to Africa to see hippos," said Miss Tam. "I'll send you postcards, just like Toot sent to Puddle."

Why did Minnie Bird screech, "Bird's-eye view"?[1] Use the word *adventure* and tell what Miss Tam wants to do.[2]

64

❶ **Understand:** Explaining, Using Idioms and Expressions—bird's-eye view (Minnie Bird said "bird's-eye view" because the map shows how the world looks when a bird flies over it.)

❷ **Understand:** Explaining—Goal; Using Vocabulary—adventure (Miss Tam wants to go on an adventure to Africa.)

★CHAPTER RETELL • BOOKMAKING

COMPREHENSION PROCESSES

Remember, Understand

WRITING TRAITS

Conventions—Period

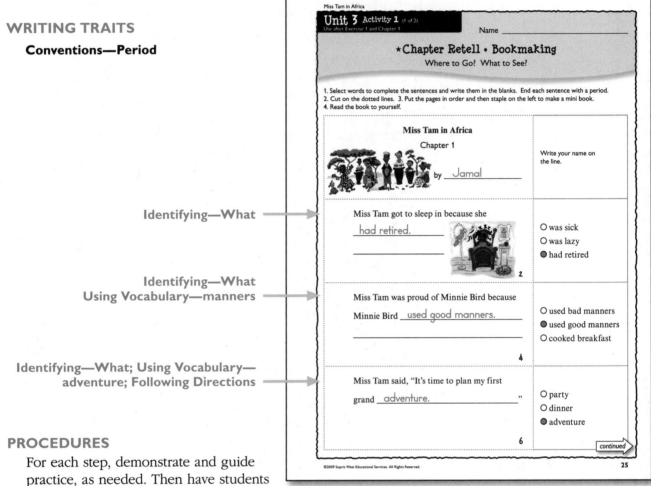

Miss Tam in Africa

Unit 3 Activity 1 (1 of 2)
Use after Exercise 1 and Chapter 1

Name _____

★**Chapter Retell • Bookmaking**
Where to Go? What to See?

1. Select words to complete the sentences and write them in the blanks. End each sentence with a period.
2. Cut on the dotted lines. 3. Put the pages in order and then staple on the left to make a mini book.
4. Read the book to yourself.

Miss Tam in Africa
Chapter 1

by Jamal

Write your name on the line.

Miss Tam got to sleep in because she
had retired.
_____

2

○ was sick
○ was lazy
● had retired

Miss Tam was proud of Minnie Bird because
Minnie Bird used good manners.
_____

4

○ used bad manners
● used good manners
○ cooked breakfast

Miss Tam said, "It's time to plan my first
grand adventure. "
_____

6

○ party
○ dinner
● adventure

continued

©2009 Sopris West Educational Services. All Rights Reserved.

25

Identifying—What

Identifying—What
Using Vocabulary—manners

Identifying—What; Using Vocabulary—
adventure; Following Directions

PROCEDURES

For each step, demonstrate and guide practice, as needed. Then have students complete the page independently.

1. **Selection Response—Specific Instructions**
   - Have students read each sentence, then fill in the bubble and blank with the correct answer.
   - Think aloud with students and discuss the multiple-choice options, as needed.
   - Remind students to put a period at the end of the sentences.

★ 2. **Bookmaking—Introductory Instructions**
   - Have students cut along the dotted lines on their Activity page.
   - Have students put the mini-book pages in order, with the title in front.
     Now put your retell book pages in order. Remember to put the page with the title first. The rest of the pages are numbered. When you have them in order, we'll staple them on the left side to make a mini-book that will retell what happened in the chapter.

   Self-monitoring
   Have students read their mini-books to make sure they make sense.

24   ★ = New in this unit

CHAPTER RETELL • BOOKMAKING (continued)

COMPREHENSION PROCESSES
Remember, Understand, Apply

WRITING TRAITS
Conventions—Period

Identifying—What
Using Vocabulary—habit, ordinary

Identifying—What

Identifying—What
Using Vocabulary—Africa

Identifying—What
Inferring; Using Vocabulary—Africa

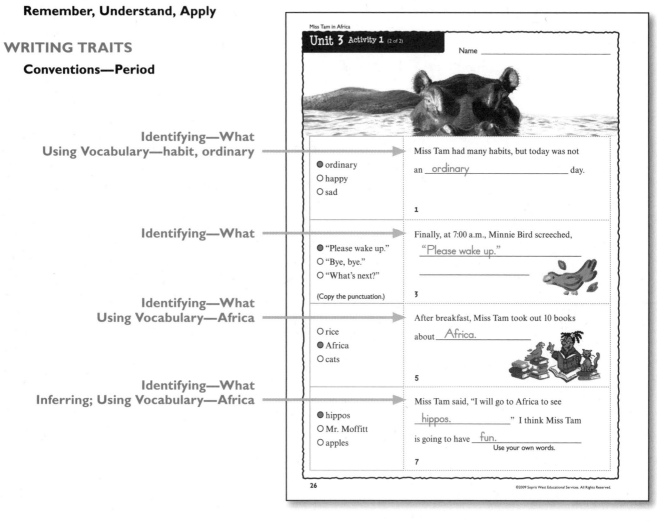

Miss Tam in Africa

Unit 3 Activity 1 (2 of 2)

Name _____

● ordinary
○ happy
○ sad

Miss Tam had many habits, but today was not an ___ordinary___ day.

1

● "Please wake up."
○ "Bye, bye."
○ "What's next?"

(Copy the punctuation.)

Finally, at 7:00 a.m., Minnie Bird screeched, "Please wake up."

_____

3

○ rice
● Africa
○ cats

After breakfast, Miss Tam took out 10 books about ___Africa.___

5

● hippos
○ Mr. Moffitt
○ apples

Miss Tam said, "I will go to Africa to see ___hippos.___" I think Miss Tam is going to have ___fun.___

Use your own words.

7

PASSAGE READING FLUENCY

FLUENCY

Accuracy, Expression, Rate

PROCEDURES

For each step, demonstrate and guide practice, as needed. Then have students complete the page independently.

Passage Reading—Basic Instructions

- Have students read the practice words.
- Have students finger track and whisper read the story two times—the first time for accuracy and the second for expression. Have students cross out a hippo each time they finish.
- Have students do a one-minute Timed Reading. Have students cross out the timer when they finish.

Say something like:

You are going to track with your finger and whisper read.

You are going to read the passage three times.

The first time, read for accuracy. What will you read for? (accuracy)

The second time, read for accuracy and expression. What will you read for?

(accuracy and expression)

Each time you read, cross out a hippo and notice how much better your reading sounds. The last time you read, use the timer. Read quickly, but accurately and with expression. See if you can finish reading before one minute is up.

Miss Tam in Africa

Unit 3 Activity 2
Use after Exercise 1 and Chapter 1

Name ______________________________

Passage Reading Fluency

1. Practice these words:

wonderful	retired	adventure	unfolded	screeched

2. Read the story 2 times. Cross out a hippo each time you read the story.

Planning an Adventure

"Oh, how wonderful to not have to get out of bed," said Miss Tam. 14
It was a new day, not an ordinary day. Miss Tam was retired, and she 29
could sleep in. 32

"Seeds, please. Seeds, please," Minnie Bird screeched. Miss Tam 41
smiled. Minnie Bird had good manners. 47

As was her habit, Miss Tam popped out of bed, put on her slippers, 61
and slipped into her old blue robe. Old Scraggly Cat just opened and 74
closed one eye. 77

Miss Tam looked at the unfolded map and books on Africa. She 89
was set to plan her first adventure. Like Toot, she would go to Africa 103
and see the hippos. What an adventure it would be! 113

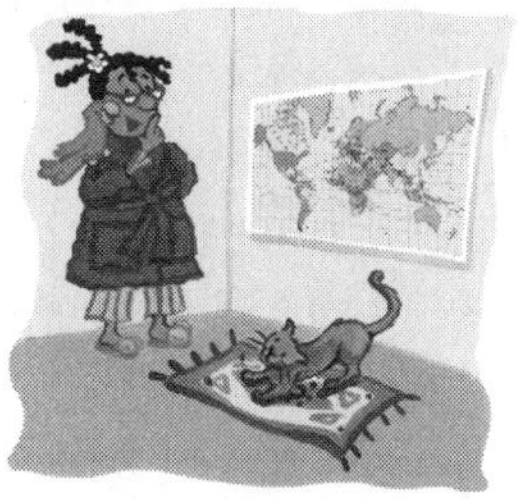

3. Set a timer and see how far you can read in one minute.
Then cross out the timer

27

ACCURACY PRECEDES RATE
(Reminder)

Students should read the story with a high degree of accuracy before proceeding to Timed Readings. Reading for increased rate before establishing a high degree of accuracy may encourage students to guess at words.

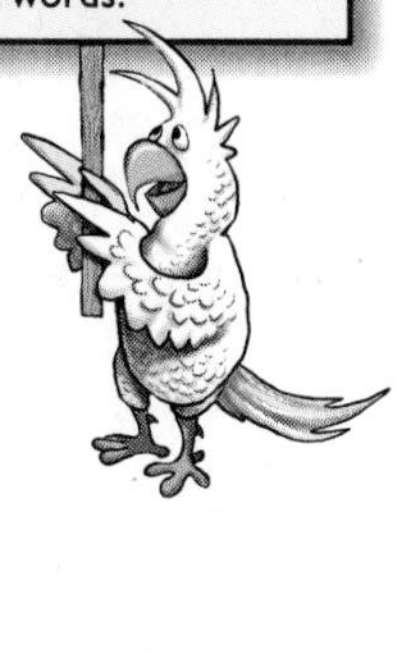

① SOUND REVIEW

Have students read the sounds and key word phrases.

Work for accuracy, then fluency.

Read the sounds and the phrases.

(/ōō/ as in blue, /ŏŏ/ as in crew, /aw/ as in paw, /ēēē/ as in baby)

PACING

Exercise 2a should take about 10 minutes, allowing about 10 minutes for the Partner Reading Focus Lesson.

② SHIFTY WORD BLENDING

For each word, have students say the underlined sound. Then have them sound out the word smoothly and say it. Use the words in sentences, as needed.

③ SOUND PRACTICE

- For each task, have students spell and say the focus sound in the gray bar.
- Next, have students read each underlined sound, the word, then the whole column.
- For the Bossy E Column, read the header, then have students identify whether the Bossy E is on the end of the word. Have students identify the underlined sound and then read the word.
- Repeat with each column, building accuracy first, then fluency.

④ ACCURACY AND FLUENCY BUILDING

- For each task, have students say any underlined part, then read the word.
- Set a pace. Then have students read the whole words in each task and column.
- Provide repeated practice, building accuracy first, then fluency.

E1. Tricky Words

- For each Tricky Word, have students identify known sounds or word parts. Use the word in a sentence to help with pronunciation.
- If the word is unfamiliar, tell students the word. Then have students say, spell, and say it.

shoes

Try to sound out the first Tricky Word in your head.

Thumbs up when you know the word. Use my sentence to help you pronounce the word.

On my feet, I wear socks and . . . *shoes.* Spell *shoes.* (s-h-o-e-s)

Read the word three times. (shoes, shoes, shoes)

worry	If you think something bad might happen, you might . . . *worry.*
half	I don't want a whole sandwich. Please cut it in . . . *half.*
library	Todd likes to check out books from the . . . *library.*

⑤ MULTISYLLABIC WORDS

For each word, have students read each syllable, finger count, then read the whole word. Use the word in a sentence, as appropriate.

travel	2 syllables	My family likes to go on trips. We like to . . . *travel.*
visit	2 syllables	My aunt and uncle are coming over to . . . *visit.*
goodbye	2 syllables	Before Jasmine left the party, she told everyone . . . *goodbye.*
bittersweet	3 syllables	If something is sad and happy at the same time, it's . . . *bittersweet.*

⑥ MORPHOGRAPHS

- Have students read "un equals not" and the accompanying word and sentence.
- Then have students explain the sentence. Say something like:
  What does "I left the door unlocked" mean? (I didn't lock the door.)

Miss Tam in Africa

Unit 3 Exercise 2a
Use before Exercise 2b (Focus Lesson)

1. **SOUND REVIEW** Have students review sounds for accuracy, then for fluency.

Ⓐ	ue as in blue	ew as in crew	aw as in paw	-y as in baby

Ⓑ	i_e	igh	ay	o_e	ea	ch

2. **SHIFTY WORD BLENDING** For each word, have students say the underlined part, sound out smoothly, then read the word.

<u>sea</u>	<u>tea</u>	<u>tea</u>r	t<u>o</u>re	<u>m</u>ore

3. **SOUND PRACTICE** In each column, have students spell and say the sound, then say any underlined sound and the word. Next, have students read the whole column.

ue	ew	i	aw	Bossy E
bl<u>ue</u>	n<u>ew</u>	st<u>i</u>ff	l<u>aw</u>n	c<u>a</u>r
tr<u>ue</u>	fl<u>ew</u>	th<u>i</u>n	d<u>aw</u>n	c<u>a</u>re
cl<u>ue</u>	gr<u>ew</u>	p<u>i</u>n	dr<u>aw</u>	T<u>i</u>m
		hatp<u>i</u>n		t<u>i</u>me

4. **ACCURACY AND FLUENCY BUILDING** For each column, have students say any underlined part, then read each word. Next, have students read the whole column.

A1 Mixed Practice	B1 Rhyming Words	C1 Names and Places	D1 Word Endings	E1 Tricky Words
sturd<u>y</u>	all	Mr. Moffitt	<u>tired</u>	shoes
d<u>a</u>rk	tall	Ghana	<u>later</u>	worry
c<u>ou</u>ch	stall	Africa	<u>toddled</u>	half
<u>a</u>way	old		<u>reached</u>	library
wh<u>i</u>le	bold		<u>parting</u>	people
cr<u>aw</u>led	fold			country
p<u>ou</u>ted				welcome

5. **MULTISYLLABIC WORDS** Have students read and finger count each word part, then read each whole word.

Ⓐ	trav•el	travel	vis•it	visit

Ⓑ	good•bye	goodbye	bit•ter•sweet	bitterweet

6. **MORPHOGRAPHS** Have students practice reading "un = not" and the related word and sentence.

un = not   unlocked = not locked   I left the door <u>unlocked</u>.

17

BUILDING MASTERY (Reminder)

For each task, have students work first on accuracy and then on fluency. Have fun! Practice words multiple times in varied ways. Have students whisper the words, squeak the words, and read the sounds and words in a rhythm.

GENTLE CORRECTIONS

If you hear an error, write the word on the board.

Have all students identify the difficult sound and then blend the word.

Periodically, repeat practice of the difficult word.

FOCUS LESSON
Skills and Strategies

★ PARTNER READING

PURPOSE

Partner Reading provides important practice and also teaches students to work productively with another student. Study the script in advance of instruction so you can visualize how to teach Partner Reading. Do not read the script during instruction.

❶ PARTNER READING INTRODUCTION

- Introduce Partner Reading.

  Today, you're going to learn how to do Partner Reading. Partner Reading is a great way to improve your expression and fluency in reading. Great football players practice the same play over and over so they can use it successfully in a game. Great readers do the same thing—they practice.

- Have students read the Partner Reading expectations.

  Let's read how we will do Partner Reading in this group. Look at your book. Put your finger on the first sentence. Let's read the expectations. (Sit side by side. Lay books open and flat. Finger track. Read quietly. Compliment your partner.)

- Have two students demonstrate the procedures as students guide them.

  [Katisha] and [Ricardo], please bring your books and stand next to me.

  Everyone, read the first sentence again. (Sit side by side.)

  [Katisha] and [Ricardo], sit like this. **Place students side by side.**

  Everyone, are they sitting side by side? (yes)

- Repeat with "lay books open and flat."
- Have the students demonstrate Partner Reading using the paragraph on page 18 in *Exercise Book 1*.

  Everyone, watch [Ricardo] and [Katisha] do Partner Reading.

  [Ricardo] is going to track each word [Katisha] reads.

  What kind of voice will [Katisha] use? (a quiet voice)

  Yes, our Partner Reading expectations say to "read quietly."

- After the students demonstrate Partner Reading, verify each expectation.

  Everyone, did [Ricardo] and [Katisha] sit side by side and lay their books flat? (yes)

  Everyone, did [Ricardo] follow every word [Katisha] read? (yes)

  Did [Katisha] read quietly? (yes)

  Now what does Ricardo need to do? (Compliment [Katisha].)

  Ricardo, what can you tell Katisha? (nice job)

  That's right. You could also say "Katisha, you read with great expression." Now it will be [Ricardo's] turn to read.

❷ PARTNER READING PRACTICE

- Have student pairs sit at designated *partner stations*. Assign seats and/or mark locations with tape or signs.
- Monitor and provide positive feedback as children practice.
- Guide daily Partner Reading until students are successful without supervision. Then assign Partner Reading as part of independent work.

Miss Tam in Africa

Unit 3 Exercise 2b (Focus Lesson)
Use after Exercise 2a and before Chapter 2

Partner Reading

PARTNER READING EXPECTATIONS

Sit side by side.

Lay books open and flat.

Finger track.

Read quietly.

Compliment your partner.

Let's Practice!

Where in the world is Miss Tam going? She is going on a great adventure. She hopes to meet new people and see hippos. Miss Tam is going to Africa!

When Miss Tam leaves for Africa, it will be bittersweet. Minnie Bird and Scraggly Cat will have to stay behind. Miss Tam will miss her pets, but she will send them postcards.

CHAPTER 2 INSTRUCTIONS
Students read with the teacher.

COMPREHENSION PROCESSES
Remember, Understand, Apply

PROCEDURES

1. Reviewing Chapter 1

   **Describing—Main Character; Locating Information;
   Using Vocabulary—habit, adventure**

   You read Chapter 1. Let's talk about what you learned about Miss Tam.
   Go back to page 62. Look at the pictures for ideas. You may also want to
   quickly review parts of the story. What do you remember about Miss Tam?
   (She gets up at the same time, even though she's retired. She has many habits.
   Minnie Bird and Scraggly Cat are her pets. She likes to read. She is going on
   an adventure.)

2. Introducing Chapter 2

   Identifying—Title
   Have students identify the title. Ask the gray text questions under the title
   to introduce the chapter.

3. First Reading
   • Ask questions and discuss the story, as indicated by the gray text.
   • Mix group and individual turns, independent of your voice.
     Have students work toward a group accuracy goal of 0–3 errors.
     Quietly keep track of errors made by all students in the group.
   • After reading the story, practice any difficult words.
     Reread the story if students have not reached the accuracy goal.

4. Second Reading, Timed Readings: Repeated Reading

      • As time allows, have students do Timed Readings while others
       follow along.
      • Time individuals for 30 seconds and encourage each child to
   work for a personal best.
   • Determine words correct per minute. Record student scores.

★ **5. Partner Reading or Whisper Reading: Repeated Reading, Chapter 2**

   Before beginning independent work, have students finger track
   and partner or whisper read. For Partner Reading, follow the
   expectations outlined in the previous Focus Lesson.

6. Homework 2: Repeated Reading

★ = New in this unit

MISS TAM IN AFRICA

Chapter 2

The Dark Blue Hatpin

What does Miss Tam want to do?[1]
I wonder why this chapter is called "The Dark Blue Hatpin."[2]

The next day, Miss Tam went to visit her old friend Mr. Moffitt.

Miss Tam put on her sturdy brown walking shoes and walked three blocks to the bus stop. She reached the library in time to have lunch with Mr. Moffitt. It was like old times.

Miss Tam said, "I am going to Africa. I will send you postcards."

What is Miss Tam doing?[3] Why is it like old times?[4]

65

COMPREHENDING AS YOU GO

❶ **Understand:** Explaining—Goal; Using Vocabulary—Africa (She wants to go to Africa to see the hippos.)

❷ **Apply:** Predicting (It will be about a hatpin . . .)

❸ **Understand:** Explaining—What (She is having lunch with Mr. Moffitt.)

❹ **Apply:** Inferring, Explaining (It's like old times because when she worked, she had lunch with Mr. Moffitt every day.)

WITH THE TEACHER

Mr. Moffitt said, "Oh my, Miss Tam, Africa is a very big continent. You must go to the country of Ghana. There, my dear friend Kwesi (Kwe-see) will welcome you. He will take you to see amazing things!"

When Miss Tam got home, she took out a dark blue hatpin and stuck it into the country of Ghana. "I am going to Ghana, Minnie Bird."

Old Scraggly Cat crawled under the couch and pouted.

Why is this chapter called "The Dark Blue Hatpin"?**1** Where is Miss Tam going to go?**2** What did Old Scraggly Cat do?**3**

66

COMPREHENDING AS YOU GO

❶ **Apply:** Inferring (It's called "The Dark Blue Hatpin" because that's what Miss Tam sticks on the map to show where she is going.)

❷ **Remember:** Identifying—Where; Using Vocabulary—Ghana (She is going to Ghana.)

❸ **Remember:** Identifying—What; Using Vocabulary—pout (Old Scraggly Cat crawled under the couch and pouted.)

MISS TAM IN AFRICA

"Don't worry. Mr. Moffitt will take good care of you while I am away," said Miss Tam.

Soon Miss Tam's new travel bag was packed. With a tear in her eye, she said goodbye to her friends. Parting was bittersweet.

A day and a half later, a stiff and tired Miss Tam toddled off the plane into a sea of people. She was in Ghana!

Why was parting bittersweet?**1** Why was Miss Tam stiff and tired when she toddled off the plane in *Ghana*?**2** Who can show me how to toddle? Let's all try it.**3**

67

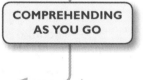

COMPREHENDING AS YOU GO

1 **Apply:** Inferring; Using Vocabulary—bittersweet (It was bittersweet because Miss Tam was sad to leave her friends, but happy to go to Ghana.)

2 **Apply:** Inferring, Explaining (She is stiff and tired because it took a day and a half to get to Ghana.)

3 **Apply:** Demonstrating

STORY COMPREHENSION

COMPREHENSION PROCESSES

Remember, Understand

WRITING TRAITS

Conventions—Period

Identifying—Main Character →

Identifying—What →

Identifying—What →

Identifying—What →

Identifying—What; Using Vocabulary— popular, ordinary, bittersweet →

Identifying—What →

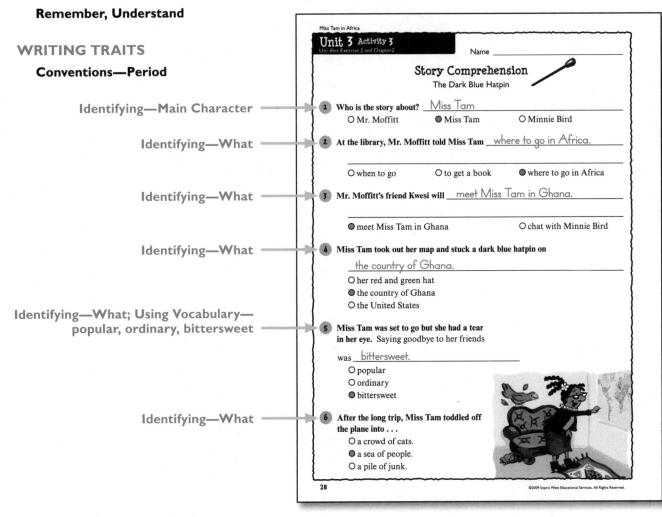

Miss Tam in Africa

Unit 3 Activity 3
Use after Exercise 2 and Chapter 2

Name _____

Story Comprehension
The Dark Blue Hatpin

1. **Who is the story about?** Miss Tam
   ○ Mr. Moffitt   ● Miss Tam   ○ Minnie Bird

2. **At the library, Mr. Moffitt told Miss Tam** where to go in Africa.
   _____
   ○ when to go   ○ to get a book   ● where to go in Africa

3. **Mr. Moffitt's friend Kwesi will** meet Miss Tam in Ghana.
   _____
   ● meet Miss Tam in Ghana   ○ chat with Minnie Bird

4. **Miss Tam took out her map and stuck a dark blue hatpin on**
   the country of Ghana.
   ○ her red and green hat
   ● the country of Ghana
   ○ the United States

5. **Miss Tam was set to go but she had a tear in her eye. Saying goodbye to her friends**
   was bittersweet.
   ○ popular
   ○ ordinary
   ● bittersweet

6. **After the long trip, Miss Tam toddled off the plane into . . .**
   ○ a crowd of cats.
   ● a sea of people.
   ○ a pile of junk.

28   ©2009 Sopris West Educational Services. All Rights Reserved.

PROCEDURES

For each step, demonstrate and guide practice, as needed. Then have students complete the page independently.

Selection Response—Basic Instructions (Items 1–6)
- Have students read each sentence or question, then fill in the bubble and/or blank with the correct answer.
- Think aloud with students and discuss the multiple-choice options, as needed.
- Remind students to put a period at the end of the sentences.

Self-monitoring

Have students check and correct their work.

MAIN IDEA

COMPREHENSION PROCESSES

Remember, Understand, Analyze

WRITING TRAITS

Conventions—Complete Sentence, Capital, Period

Identifying—Who

Identifying—What

Classifying

Identifying—Main Idea

Visualizing, Illustrating

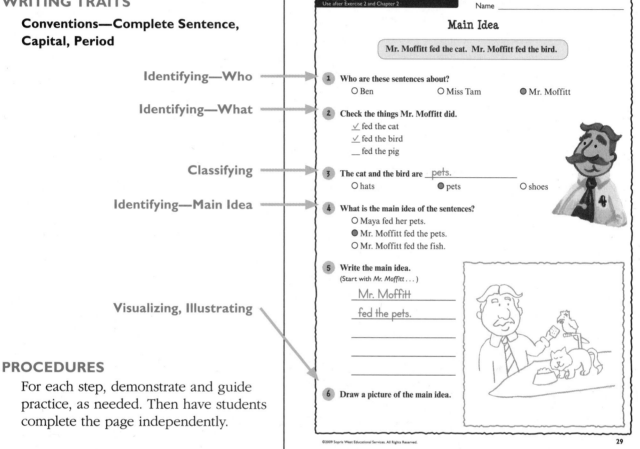

Miss Tam in Africa

Unit 3 Activity 4
Use after Exercise 2 and Chapter 2

Name _____

Main Idea

Mr. Moffitt fed the cat. Mr. Moffitt fed the bird.

1. Who are these sentences about?
   ○ Ben   ○ Miss Tam   ● Mr. Moffitt

2. Check the things Mr. Moffitt did.
   ✓ fed the cat
   ✓ fed the bird
   __ fed the pig

3. The cat and the bird are _pets._
   ○ hats   ● pets   ○ shoes

4. What is the main idea of the sentences?
   ○ Maya fed her pets.
   ● Mr. Moffitt fed the pets.
   ○ Mr. Moffitt fed the fish.

5. Write the main idea.
   (Start with Mr. Moffitt . . .)
   Mr. Moffitt
   fed the pets.

6. Draw a picture of the main idea.

©2009 Sopris West Educational Services. All Rights Reserved.   29

PROCEDURES

For each step, demonstrate and guide practice, as needed. Then have students complete the page independently.

1. **Main Idea: Selection Response— Basic Instructions** (Items 1–4)
   - Have students read the sentences in the box.
   - Have students read the questions and sentence stem. Then have them check or fill in the bubble and/or blank with the correct answer.

2. **Main Idea: Sentence Writing, Illustrating—Specific Instructions** (Items 5, 6)
   - Have students write the main idea sentence. Have students read the sentence starter. Ask students how to start and end the sentence. Say something like:
     Now you're going to write the main idea. Read the sentence starter. (Mr. Moffitt . . .)
     What did Mr. Moffit do in the sentences? (fed the pets)
     How are you going to write the main idea? (Mr. Moffitt fed the pets.)
   - Then have students visualize and illustrate the main idea.
     To illustrate the main idea, I can imagine Mr. Moffitt with his mustache.
     Can you imagine what he is wearing? (a shirt and tie)
     What else needs to go in our pictures? (a cat and a bird)
     Can you imagine what the bird looks like? ([Minnie Bird])
     That's what I imagine too. Where will Minnie Bird be in your picture?
     ([on Mr. Moffitt's shoulder])
     That would be fun. What else should be in the picture?

① SOUND REVIEW

Use selected Sound Cards from Units 1–3.

★② NEW SOUND INTRODUCTION

- Tell students u_e says /o͞o/ as in flute.
- Have students look at the picture, identify "flute," and read the sentence.
  June and Luke like to play the flute.
- Have students practice: u_e says /o͞o/ as in flute.
- Have students read the sentence again, then identify the three words with /o͞o/ as in flute.
- For Row B, have students read the underlined sound, then the word.
- Have students go back and read just the words. Mix group and individual turns.

③ ACCURACY AND FLUENCY BUILDING

- For each task, have students say any underlined part, then read the word.
- Set a pace. Then have students read the whole words in each task and column.
- Provide repeated practice, building accuracy first, then fluency, independent of your voice.

C1. Multisyllabic Words

- For each word, have students read and finger count each syllable, then read the word.
  Use the word in a sentence, as appropriate.

Western	2 syllables	The cowboys wore . . . *Western* . . . clothes.
market	2 syllables	Tara's mom buys vegetables at the farmer's . . . *market.*
insult	2 syllables	Ike didn't shake Dee's hand, and Dee felt it was an . . . *insult.*
perfectly	3 syllables	You couldn't have done it any better. You did it . . . *perfectly.*
baskets	2 syllables	The eggs we collected filled two . . . *baskets.*
custom	2 syllables	Shaking hands is a . . . *custom.*
African	3 syllables	If you are from Africa, then you are . . . *African.*

E1. Tricky Words

For each Tricky Word, have students identify known sounds or word parts. Use the word
in a sentence to help with pronunciation.

full	We couldn't get into the show because it was already . . . *full.*
footwear	Shaquille sells shoes in the . . . *footwear* . . . department.
bargained	I got the price down because I . . . *bargained.*

E2. Story Words

Tell students the underlined sound, then have them read the word.

④ WORD ENDINGS

Have students read each set of words. Tell students you drop the e when you add *-ing* to
"shake" and "drive," and you change the y to i when you add *-ed* to "try."

⑤ AFFIXES

★Tell students they can already read words that begin with *ex-*. Explain that *ex-* says /ex/.
- Have students read the underlined part, then the word.

⑥ MORPHOGRAPHS

Have students read the underlined part, then the word. Then have students rephrase each word.

★ = New in this unit

Miss Tam in Africa

Unit 3 Exercise 3
Use before Chapter 3

1. SOUND REVIEW Use selected Sound Cards from Units 1–3.

★2. NEW SOUND INTRODUCTION Introduce the new sound /ōō/ as in flute.

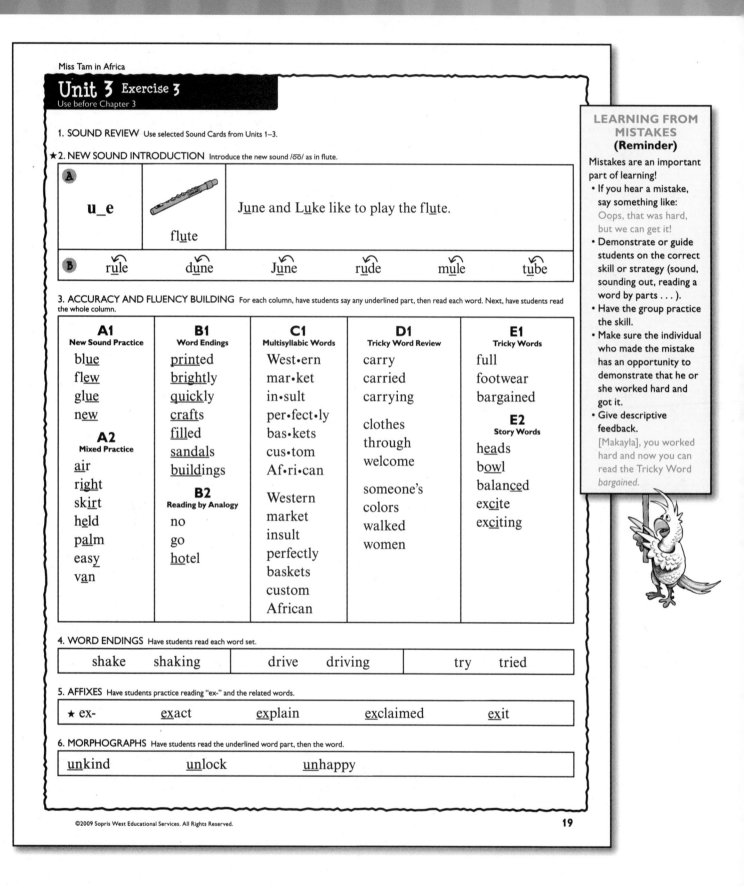

A

| u_e | flute | June and Luke like to play the flute. |

B r<u>u</u>le   d<u>u</u>ne   J<u>u</u>ne   r<u>u</u>de   m<u>u</u>le   t<u>u</u>be

3. ACCURACY AND FLUENCY BUILDING For each column, have students say any underlined part, then read each word. Next, have students read the whole column.

A1 New Sound Practice	B1 Word Endings	C1 Multisyllabic Words	D1 Tricky Word Review	E1 Tricky Words
bl<u>ue</u>	<u>print</u>ed	West•ern	carry	full
fl<u>ew</u>	<u>bright</u>ly	mar•ket	carried	footwear
gl<u>ue</u>	<u>quick</u>ly	in•sult	carrying	bargained
n<u>ew</u>	<u>craft</u>s	per•fect•ly		
	<u>fill</u>ed	bas•kets	clothes	**E2** Story Words
A2 Mixed Practice	<u>sandal</u>s	cus•tom	through	h<u>ea</u>ds
<u>ai</u>r	<u>building</u>s	Af•ri•can	welcome	b<u>ow</u>l
r<u>igh</u>t				balan<u>c</u>ed
sk<u>ir</u>t	**B2** Reading by Analogy	Western	someone's	ex<u>c</u>ite
h<u>e</u>ld	no	market	colors	ex<u>c</u>iting
p<u>al</u>m	go	insult	walked	
eas<u>y</u>	<u>ho</u>tel	perfectly	women	
v<u>a</u>n		baskets		
		custom		
		African		

4. WORD ENDINGS Have students read each word set.

shake shaking	drive driving	try tried

5. AFFIXES Have students practice reading "ex-" and the related words.

★ ex-   <u>ex</u>act   <u>ex</u>plain   <u>ex</u>claimed   <u>ex</u>it

6. MORPHOGRAPHS Have students read the underlined word part, then the word.

<u>un</u>kind   <u>un</u>lock   <u>un</u>happy

19

COMPREHENSION PROCESSES

Remember, Understand, Apply

PROCEDURES

Introducing Vocabulary

> ★ insult ★ custom
> ★ bargain ★ habitat,
> hesitate ★ wildlife
> ★ protected

- For each vocabulary word, have students read the word by parts, then read the whole word.
- Read the student-friendly explanations to students as they follow with their fingers. Then have students use the vocabulary word by following the gray text.
- Review and discuss the photos and illustrations, as appropriate.

> **USING VOCABULARY**

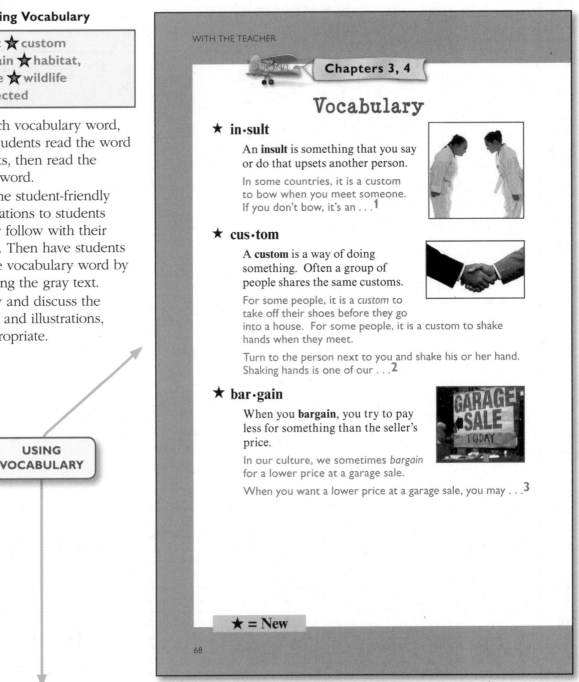

WITH THE TEACHER

Chapters 3, 4

Vocabulary

★ **in·sult**

An **insult** is something that you say or do that upsets another person.

In some countries, it is a custom to bow when you meet someone. If you don't bow, it's an . . .**1**

★ **cus·tom**

A **custom** is a way of doing something. Often a group of people shares the same customs.

For some people, it is a *custom* to take off their shoes before they go into a house. For some people, it is a custom to shake hands when they meet.

Turn to the person next to you and shake his or her hand. Shaking hands is one of our . . .**2**

★ **bar·gain**

When you **bargain**, you try to pay less for something than the seller's price.

In our culture, we sometimes *bargain* for a lower price at a garage sale.

When you want a lower price at a garage sale, you may . . .**3**

★ = New

68

---

❶ Understand: Using Vocabulary—insult (insult)

❷ Understand: Using Vocabulary—custom (customs)

❸ Remember: Using Vocabulary—bargain (bargain)

★ **hab·i·tat**

The place where an animal or plant lives and grows is called its **habitat**.

Some foxes live in the desert. What is their *habitat?*1

hes·i·tate

Hesitate means to stop before saying or doing something. You hesitate because you aren't sure what to do.

Miss Tam *hesitated* before she boarded the airplane. She wondered if this was the right flight.

Why do you think Miss Tam hesitated?2

★ **wild·life**

Animals and plants that live in their natural habitat are called **wildlife**.

Many people study the forest *wildlife*.

Name some forest wildlife.3

★ **pro·tect·ed**

When things, people, or animals are **protected**, they are kept safe from harm.

The animals in the wildlife park are *protected* from hunters.

Where else would you find animals that are protected?4

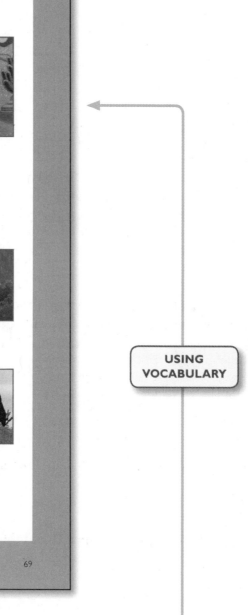

69

USING VOCABULARY

❶ **Understand:** Using Vocabulary—habitat (Their habitat is the desert.)

❷ **Apply:** Inferring; Explaining; Using Vocabulary—hesitate (Miss Tam hesitated because she wasn't sure she was getting on the right airplane . . .)

❸ **Apply:** Using Vocabulary—wildlife (Some of the forest wildlife are foxes, raccoons, bears . . .)

❹ **Apply:** Priming Background Knowledge; Using Vocabulary—protected (Animals that live in the zoo are protected . . .)

CHAPTER 3 INSTRUCTIONS
Students read with the teacher.

COMPREHENSION PROCESSES
Remember, Understand, Apply

PROCEDURES

1. **Reviewing Chapters 1 and 2**

   Identifying—Setting
   At the end of Chapter 2, where was Miss Tam?
   (She was in Ghana. She was at the airport.)

2. **Introducing Chapter 3**
   Discuss the title and main character by following the gray text under the chapter title.

3. **First Reading**
   - Ask questions and discuss the story, as indicated by the gray text.
   - Mix group and individual turns, independent of your voice.
     Have students work toward a group accuracy goal of 0–3 errors.
     Quietly keep track of errors made by all students in the group.
   - After reading the story, practice any difficult words.
     Reread the story if students have not reached the accuracy goal.

   > **CORRECTING DECODING ERRORS**
   > During story reading, gently correct any error, then have students reread the sentence.

4. **Second Reading, Short Passage Practice: Developing Prosody**
   - Demonstrate expressive, fluent reading of the first page. Read just above students' rate. Say something like:
     Listen to me read the first paragraph. "The air was hot and still. Miss Tam was in Ghana! A tall thin man held up a paper that said, 'Miss Tam.' It was Mr. Moffitt's friend Kwesi. Miss Tam walked over to Kwesi."

   - Guide practice with your voice.
     Read the first paragraph with me. (The air was hot and still . . .)

   - Provide individual turns while others track with their fingers and whisper read.
   - Repeat with one paragraph or page at a time.

5. **Partner Reading or Whisper Reading: Repeated Reading, Chapter 3**
    Before beginning independent work, have students finger track and partner or whisper read.

6. **Homework 3: Repeated Reading**

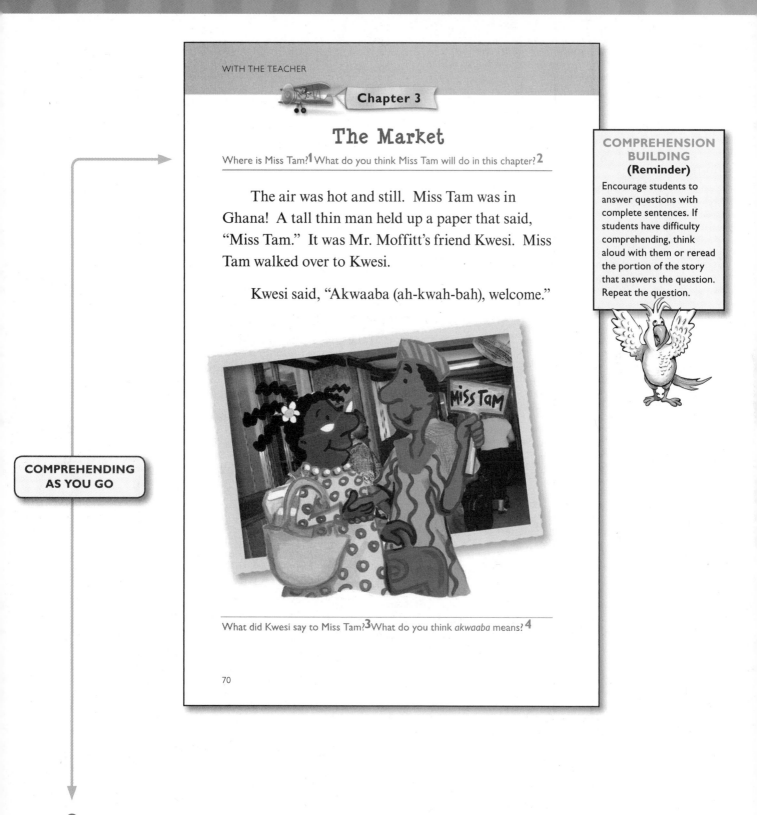

WITH THE TEACHER

Chapter 3

The Market

Where is Miss Tam?**1** What do you think Miss Tam will do in this chapter? **2**

The air was hot and still. Miss Tam was in Ghana! A tall thin man held up a paper that said, "Miss Tam." It was Mr. Moffitt's friend Kwesi. Miss Tam walked over to Kwesi.

Kwesi said, "Akwaaba (ah-kwah-bah), welcome."

What did Kwesi say to Miss Tam?**3** What do you think *akwaaba* means? **4**

70

COMPREHENSION BUILDING (Reminder)

Encourage students to answer questions with complete sentences. If students have difficulty comprehending, think aloud with them or reread the portion of the story that answers the question. Repeat the question.

COMPREHENDING AS YOU GO

❶ Remember: Identifying—Setting; Using Vocabulary—Ghana (Miss Tam is in Ghana.)

❷ Apply: Predicting (She will go to a market.)

❸ Remember: Identifying—What (Kwesi said "akwaaba" to Miss Tam.)

❹ Apply: Inferring (Akwaaba means welcome . . .)

MISS TAM IN AFRICA

Miss Tam held out her hand. She was careful to shake Kwesi's hand with her right hand. Miss Tam had learned that in Ghana it was good manners to use your right hand but an insult to shake someone's hand with your left.

Soon they were driving slowly in Kwesi's van. Miss Tam saw white buildings and palm trees from the window. She saw people in Western clothes and people in brightly printed African clothes.

"We must go to the market," Kwesi said. "There, you can see the food and crafts of my people."

At the market, Miss Tam was amazed by all the colors! As was the custom, Miss Tam bargained for a colorful skirt, a blue shirt, and African sandals.

"What fun!" exclaimed Miss Tam. She quickly took off her old shoes and put on her new African footwear.

How did Miss Tam show good manners?[1] Describe what Miss Tam saw. [2] What did she buy at the market? [3]

71

MAKING CONNECTIONS

After completing the page, say something like:

If you went to a market in Africa, what would you want to buy?

Are there any outdoor markets where you live?

COMPREHENDING AS YOU GO

1 **Understand:** Explaining (Miss Tam shook Kwesi's hand with her right hand.)

2 **Understand:** Describing, Explaining (She saw white buildings and palm trees. She saw people in African clothes and Western clothes.)

3 **Remember:** Identifying—What (Miss Tam bought a skirt, a blue shirt, and African sandals at the market.)

WITH THE TEACHER

The streets were filled with people. Women carried big baskets full of things on their heads. One woman walked by with a big bowl of eggs perfectly balanced on her head.

When Miss Tam got to her hotel room, she tried walking with her book bag on her head. She dropped it six times. It wasn't as easy as it looked!

What are some of the *customs* in Ghana?^1 What did Miss Tam try?^2 Was it easy?^3 How do you think the women of Ghana learn to balance things on their heads?^4

72

MAKING CONNECTIONS

After completing the page, you may wish to give students an opportunity to try balancing a book on their heads.

Ask students what they would need to do if they wanted to carry things on their heads.

COMPREHENDING AS YOU GO

❶ **Remember:** Explaining; Using Vocabulary—custom, Ghana (It is a custom in Ghana for women to carry baskets on their heads. Another custom is shaking hands with the right hand.)

❷ **Remember:** Identifying—What (Miss Tam tried to walk with her book bag on her head.)

❸ **Remember:** Identifying (No, it wasn't easy.)

❹ **Apply:** Inferring (They practice a lot. They start by balancing small things . . .)

STORY COMPREHENSION

COMPREHENSION PROCESSES
Remember, Understand

WRITING TRAITS
Conventions—Complete Sentence, Capital, Period

Identifying—Main Character

Identifying—What

Identifying—What

Visualizing, Illustrating

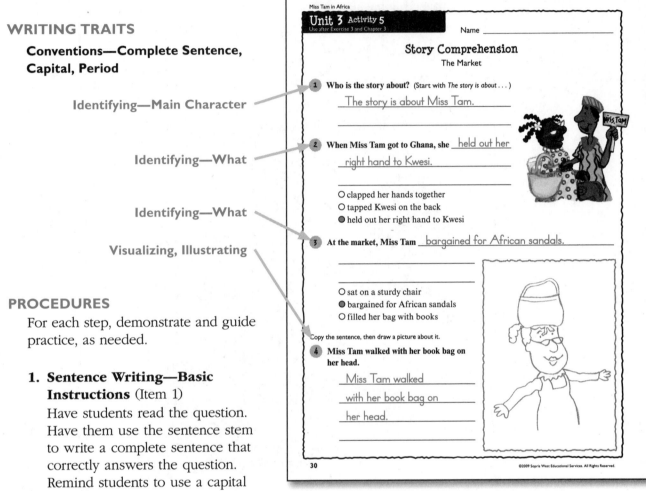

Miss Tam in Africa

Unit 3 Activity 5
Use after Exercise 3 and Chapter 3

Name _____

Story Comprehension
The Market

1 **Who is the story about?** (Start with *The story is about . . .*)

The story is about Miss Tam.

_____

2 **When Miss Tam got to Ghana, she** held out her
right hand to Kwesi.

_____

○ clapped her hands together
○ tapped Kwesi on the back
● held out her right hand to Kwesi

3 **At the market, Miss Tam** bargained for African sandals.

_____

_____

○ sat on a sturdy chair
● bargained for African sandals
○ filled her bag with books

Copy the sentence, then draw a picture about it.

4 **Miss Tam walked with her book bag on her head.**

Miss Tam walked
with her book bag on
her head.

30   ©2009 Sopris West Educational Services. All Rights Reserved.

PROCEDURES
For each step, demonstrate and guide practice, as needed.

1. **Sentence Writing—Basic Instructions** (Item 1)
   Have students read the question. Have them use the sentence stem to write a complete sentence that correctly answers the question. Remind students to use a capital letter and a period.

2. **Selection Response—Basic Instructions** (Items 2, 3)
   • Have students read each sentence stem, then fill in the bubble and/or blank.
   • Think aloud with students and discuss the multiple-choice options, as needed.
   • Remind students to put a period at the end of each sentence.

3. **Sentence Copying, Illustrating—Specific Instructions** (Item 4)
   Have students read, then copy the sentence. Remind them to start with a capital and end with a period. Then have students illustrate the sentence.
   After students read the sentence, say something like: Close your eyes and imagine Miss Tam walking with books on her head. I see Miss Tam with her funny ponytail. She has five books on her head. She is holding her arms straight out trying to balance. What do you see?

   It might be hard to draw what we are imagining. So I'm going to start with a stick figure. First I'll draw Miss Tam's head, then a stick for her body. Her arms will be one line sticking out. Her legs will be straight. **Draw a stick figure.**
   Now I can outline Miss Tam, draw her ponytail, add clothes . . . **Demonstrate how to outline Miss Tam and add details.**

VOCABULARY and ALPHABETICAL ORDER

COMPREHENSION PROCESSES
Remember, Understand, Apply

WRITING TRAITS
Conventions—Period

Alphabetical Order ⟶

Defining and Using Vocabulary—
adventure; Visualizing; Illustrating

Defining and Using Vocabulary—custom
Visualizing; Illustrating

Defining and Using Vocabulary—sturdy
Visualizing; Illustrating

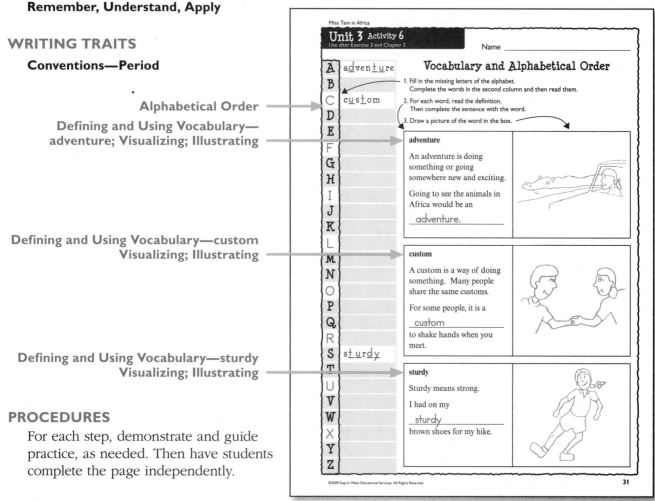

Miss Tam in Africa

Unit 3 Activity 6
Use after Exercise 3 and Chapter 3

Name _____

Vocabulary and Alphabetical Order

1. Fill in the missing letters of the alphabet.
   Complete the words in the second column and then read them.

2. For each word, read the definition.
   Then complete the sentence with the word.

3. Draw a picture of the word in the box.

A | adventure
B
C | custom
D
E
...
S | sturdy

adventure

An adventure is doing something or going somewhere new and exciting.

Going to see the animals in Africa would be an ___adventure.___

custom

A custom is a way of doing something. Many people share the same customs.

For some people, it is a ___custom___ to shake hands when you meet.

sturdy

Sturdy means strong.

I had on my ___sturdy___ brown shoes for my hike.

©2009 Sopris West Educational Services. All Rights Reserved. 31

PROCEDURES
For each step, demonstrate and guide practice, as needed. Then have students complete the page independently.

Alphabetical Order—Specific Instructions
- Have students point to and read the letters in the alphabet column and fill in the missing letters.

  Say the letters in alphabetical order. (A, B . . . C) Write C in the blank space.

- Tell students that the words in the column are in alphabetical order. Have them complete the spelling of the words by filling in the blanks.

Vocabulary: Sentence Completion, Illustrating—Specific Instructions
- Have students read the vocabulary words and definitions.
- Have students read the sample sentence and fill in the blank with the vocabulary word. Then have them visualize how to draw a picture to illustrate the word or sentence.
  Say something like:

  Going to see the animals in Africa would be an adventure. Close your eyes and imagine yourself in Africa. I can imagine seeing zebras and elephants. I think that's what I will draw for *adventure*. What animals can you imagine seeing on an African adventure?

Self-monitoring
Have students check and correct their work.

❶ SOUND REVIEW

Have students read the sounds and key word phrases. Work for accuracy, then fluency.

Read the sounds and the phrases. (/o͞o/ as in blue, /ir/ as in bird, /aw/ as in paw, /āāā/ as in rain)

❷ SHIFTY WORD BLENDING

For each word, have students say the underlined sound. Then have them sound out the word smoothly and say it. Use the words in sentences, as appropriate.

❸ ACCURACY AND FLUENCY BUILDING

• For each task, have students say any underlined part, then read the word.
• Set a pace. Then have students read the whole words in each task and column.
• Provide repeated practice, building accuracy first, then fluency, independent of your voice.

E1. Tricky Words

For each Tricky Word, have students identify known sounds or word parts. Use the word in a sentence to help with pronunciation.

hours	Our school day is about six . . . *hours*.
love	The family got a new puppy. They all . . . *love* . . . the puppy.
early	I don't like to be late, so I get up . . . *early*.
friendly	Minnie Bird is very . . . *friendly*.
only	There was just one apple left. There was . . . *only* one.
laughed	The puppy was funny. We all . . . *laughed*.

E2. Story Words

Tell students the underlined sound, then have them read the word.

❹ READING BY ANALOGY

Have students figure out how to say *o-* by reading other words they know.

❺ MULTISYLLABIC WORDS

For each word, have students read each syllable and then read the whole word. Use the word in a sentence, as appropriate.

evening	It gets dark outside in the . . . *evening*.
peppers	Emma ate some chili with hot . . . *peppers*.
habitat	For many animals, the rain forest is their . . . *habitat*.
postcard	My friend sent me a . . . *postcard*.
suddenly	The firecracker went off . . . *suddenly*.
hesitated	I was afraid to jump into the cold water, so I . . . *hesitated*.

❻ WORDS IN CONTEXT

• Tell students to use the sounds and word parts they know and then the sentence to figure out how to say each word. Assist, as needed.
• Have students read each word part, the whole word, and then the sentence.

You can use the sounds you know to figure out words.

Look at the first word in Row A. Thumbs up when you know the word.

Now read the sentence. (Miss Tam went to Africa to see the wildlife.)

Everyone, what's the underlined word? (wildlife)

Miss Tam in Africa

Unit 3 Exercise 4
Use before Chapter 4

1. SOUND REVIEW Have students review sounds for accuracy, then for fluency.

Ⓐ	ue as in blue	ir as in bird	aw as in paw	ai as in rain
Ⓑ	ou	igh	or	u_e	ew	ay

2. SHIFTY WORD BLENDING For each word, have students say the underlined part, sound out smoothly, then read the word.

b<u>ea</u>ns	<u>m</u>eans	mea<u>t</u>s	m<u>ee</u>ts

3. ACCURACY AND FLUENCY BUILDING For each column, have students say any underlined part, then read each word. Next, have students read the whole column.

A1 New Sound Practice	B1 Buildups	C1 Bossy E	D1 Word Endings	E1 Tricky Words
m<u>u</u>le	care	<u>ate</u>	<u>rented</u>	hours
t<u>u</u>ne	careful	wr<u>ote</u>	<u>filled</u>	love
t<u>u</u>be	carefully	dr<u>ive</u>	<u>traveled</u>	early
pr<u>u</u>ne		h<u>ome</u>	<u>monkeys</u>	friendly
	ray	arr<u>ive</u>	<u>arrived</u>	only
A2 Mixed Practice	gray	m<u>ore</u>	<u>hired</u>	laughed
f<u>ew</u>		gu<u>ide</u>	<u>waded</u>	
<u>agreed</u>	press		<u>used</u>	**E2** Story Words
<u>lumps</u>	impress	**C2** Places		b<u>oa</u>t
riv<u>er</u>	impressed	Montgomery	drive	rice
nev<u>er</u>		USA	driving	b<u>owl</u>
f<u>or</u>est		Alabama		

4. READING BY ANALOGY Have students figure out the underlined parts by reading other words they know.

no	go	b<u>o</u>th	h<u>o</u>tel	hipp<u>o</u>	pr<u>o</u>tect

5. MULTISYLLABIC WORDS Have students read each word part, then read each whole word.

Ⓐ	eve·ning	evening	pep·pers	peppers
Ⓑ	hab·i·tat	habitat	post·card	postcard
Ⓒ	sud·den·ly	suddenly	hes·i·tat·ed	hesitated

6. WORDS IN CONTEXT Have students use the sounds and word parts they know and then the sentence to pronounce each underlined word.

Ⓐ	wild·life	Miss Tam went to Africa to see the <u>wildlife</u>.
Ⓑ	on·ions	I cry when I cut <u>onions</u>.
Ⓒ	to·ma·toes	I went to the garden and picked red <u>tomatoes</u>.

CHAPTER 4 INSTRUCTIONS
Students read with the teacher.

COMPREHENSION PROCESSES
Remember, Understand, Apply, Analyze

PROCEDURES

1. Reviewing Chapters 1–3

> **Summarizing; Identifying—Main Character, Traits, Goal, Setting, Action; Using Vocabulary—Africa, continent, Ghana, wildlife**

Have students review Chapters 1–3 by discussing and describing the main character, what she wanted at the beginning of the story, and what happened in the middle of the story. Say something like:

Who is the main character? (Miss Tam)

What do we know about her? (She's a retired librarian. She has a bird and a cat for pets.)

At the beginning of the story, what did Miss Tam want to do? (She wanted to go on a trip.)

Where did she go? (She went to Africa. She went to Ghana.)

Yes, she went to the continent of . . . Africa . . . and the country of . . . Ghana.

What did Miss Tam do in Ghana? (She bargained for shoes, she went to a wildlife park . . .)

2. Introducing Chapter 4

> **Identifying—Title**

Have students identify the title. Ask the gray text questions to introduce the chapter.

3. First Reading

- Ask questions and discuss the story as indicated by the gray text.
- Mix group and individual turns, independent of your voice.
  Have students work toward a group accuracy goal of 0–4 errors.
  Quietly keep track of errors made by all students in the group.
- After reading the story, practice any difficult words.
  Reread the story if students have not reached the accuracy goal.

4. Second Reading, Timed Readings: Repeated Reading

- As time allows, have students do Timed Readings while others follow along.
- Time individuals for 30 seconds and encourage each child to work for a personal best.
- Count the number of words read correctly in 30 seconds (words read minus errors). Multiply by two to determine words correct per minute. Record student scores.

5. Partner Reading or Whisper Reading: Repeated Reading

Before beginning independent work, have students finger track and partner or whisper read.

6. Homework 4: Repeated Reading

MISS TAM IN AFRICA

Chapter 4

Hippos on the River

What has Miss Tam seen in Ghana so far?**1** What do you think she will do in this chapter?**2**

That evening, Miss Tam ate a rice dish that was filled with meat, onions, tomatoes, and peppers. Rice in Ghana was different from the red beans and rice Miss Tam ate at home.

Kwesi arrived early the next morning. "What do you want to see today?" he asked.

Miss Tam took *Toot and Puddle* from her bag and said, "I want to see hippos."

COMPREHENDING AS YOU GO

What did Miss Tam eat in Ghana?**3** How was it the same as eating at home? How was it different?**4** What did Miss Tam want to see?**5**

73

❶ **Understand:** Summarizing (She saw the market. She saw women carrying baskets on their heads.)

❷ **Apply:** Predicting (She will go see the hippos in the river . . .)

❸ **Remember:** Identifying—What (Miss Tam ate a rice dish that was filled with meat, onions, tomatoes, and peppers.)

❹ **Analyze:** Comparing/Contrasting; **Apply:** Using Vocabulary—Ghana (Miss Tam ate rice in Ghana like she does at home. At home, she eats rice with red beans. In Ghana, she ate rice with meat, onions, and peppers.)

❺ **Remember:** Identifying—Goal (Miss Tam wanted to see hippos.)

WITH THE TEACHER

Kwesi laughed. "Miss Tam, I have never seen a hippo in Ghana!" Kwesi hesitated, then said, "We will both have an adventure. We can go to a park where wildlife is protected. We might see the only hippos left in Ghana."

In the van, Miss Tam wrote a postcard.

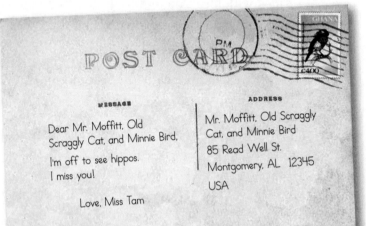

POST CARD

MESSAGE

Dear Mr. Moffitt, Old Scraggly Cat, and Minnie Bird,

I'm off to see hippos. I miss you!

Love, Miss Tam

ADDRESS

Mr. Moffitt, Old Scraggly Cat, and Minnie Bird
85 Read Well St.
Montgomery, AL 12345
USA

After driving for many hours, Kwesi and Miss Tam arrived at the wildlife park. They hired a guide and rented a boat. Then they set off down the river to see some hippos.

What are Kwesi and Miss Tam doing?[1] Why did Kwesi say, "We will both have an adventure"?[2]

74

FOCUS ON CHARACTER

Inferring— Character Traits

After completing the page, say something like:

Kwesi had never seen a hippo before, but he was happy to take Miss Tam to a wildlife park.

What do you think Kwesi thinks of Miss Tam?

Why do you think Kwesi likes Miss Tam? (She is interested in everything. She is respectful . . . appreciative . . . easy to be around . . .)

COMPREHENDING AS YOU GO

❶ **Understand:** Explaining; Using Vocabulary—wildlife (Miss Tam and Kwesi are going to the wildlife park to see the hippos.)

❷ **Apply:** Inferring; Using Vocabulary—adventure (He has never seen a hippo, so it will be an adventure for him to see them.)

WITH THE TEACHER

Suddenly, Kwesi shouted, "Look! There!" Big gray lumps sat in the water. The guide said, "Hippos seem friendly, but they can be very mean. We must stay back."

To stay cool, the hippos waded in the mud and water. The guide said, "There used to be many hippos in Ghana. Now there are only a few hundred hippos because they have lost their habitat. If we are not careful, there will be no more hippos in Ghana."

Why do you think Kwesi had never seen a hippo before? [1]

76

COMPREHENDING AS YOU GO

❶ **Apply:** Inferring; Using Vocabulary—Ghana (Kwesi has never seen a hippo because there aren't many left in Ghana.)

MISS TAM IN AFRICA

Kwesi and Miss Tam agreed that it would be very sad if there were no more hippos in Ghana.

FOCUS ON VOCABULARY— adventure

After completing the page, say something like:
I think Miss Tam is on a great *adventure*. Why do you think Miss Tam's trip is an adventure?

Hippos are endangered. That means there are very few hippos left in the world.

77

MAIN IDEA

COMPREHENSION PROCESSES

Remember, Understand, Apply, Analyze

WRITING TRAITS

Conventions—Complete Sentence, Capital, Period

Identifying—Who

Identifying—What

Classifying

Inferring—Main Idea
Using Vocabulary—wildlife

Visualizing; Illustrating

PROCEDURES

For each step, demonstrate and guide practice, as needed. Then have students complete the page independently.

1. **Main Idea: Selection Response— Specific Instructions** (Items 1–3)

   • Have students review what a main idea is. Say something like:

   Remember, a main idea tells us who or what the . . . **sentences are about.** It also tells the most important thing . . . **that is happening.**

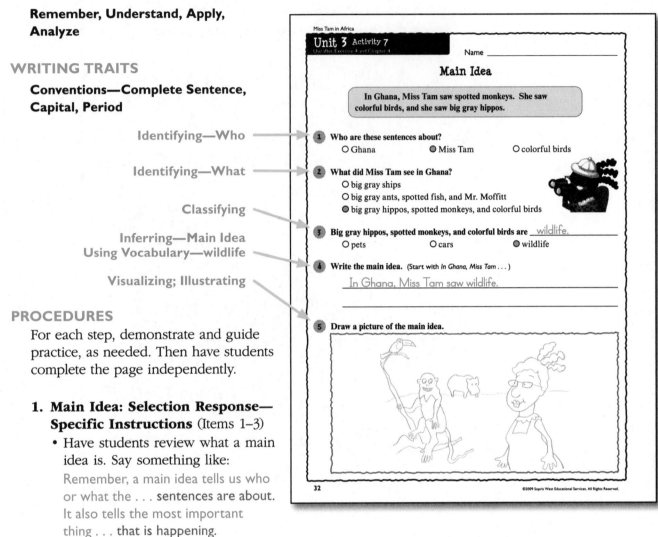

Miss Tam in Africa

Unit 3 Activity 7
Use after Exercise 4 and Chapter 4

Name _____

Main Idea

In Ghana, Miss Tam saw spotted monkeys. She saw colorful birds, and she saw big gray hippos.

1 **Who are these sentences about?**
   ○ Ghana   ● Miss Tam   ○ colorful birds

2 **What did Miss Tam see in Ghana?**
   ○ big gray ships
   ○ big gray ants, spotted fish, and Mr. Moffitt
   ● big gray hippos, spotted monkeys, and colorful birds

3 **Big gray hippos, spotted monkeys, and colorful birds are** ___wildlife.___
   ○ pets   ○ cars   ● wildlife

4 **Write the main idea.** (Start with *In Ghana, Miss Tam . . .*)

   In Ghana, Miss Tam saw wildlife.

   _____

5 **Draw a picture of the main idea.**

32   ©2009 Sopris West Educational Services. All Rights Reserved.

   • Have students read the sentences in the gray box.

   • Have students read the questions and/or sentence stem, then fill in the bubble and/or blank with the correct answer.

2. **Main Idea: Sentence Writing, Illustrating—Specific Instructions** (Items 4, 5)

   • Have students write the main idea sentence. Have students read the sentence starter.

   Look at the small print in the parentheses. How are you going to start your main idea sentence? (In Ghana, Miss Tam . . .)

   That's right. When you write, be sure to put in the comma because it tells the reader when to pause. You're going to write "In Ghana, Miss Tam . . ." What did Miss Tam do in the sentences? (saw wildlife) Nice job. You used the word *wildlife* to tell about all the things she saw. So your sentence will say . . . In Ghana, Miss Tam saw wildlife.

   • Then have students visualize and illustrate the main idea.

   To illustrate the main idea, I can imagine Miss Tam sitting in the boat watching birds.

   Can you imagine what she is wearing? (a T-shirt, jeans, and a hat)

   What else would she have? (binoculars) You are all going to have great illustrations! Where can you look if you aren't sure how to draw Miss Tam? (in our books)

PASSAGE READING FLUENCY

FLUENCY

Accuracy, Expression, Rate

PROCEDURES

For each step, demonstrate and guide practice, as needed. Then have students complete the page independently.

Passage Reading—Basic Instructions

- Have students read the practice words.
- Have students finger track and whisper read the story two times—the first time for accuracy and the second for expression. Have students cross out a hippo each time they finish.
- Have students do a one-minute Timed Reading. Have students cross out the timer when they finish. Say something like:

You are going to track with your finger and whisper read.

You are going to read the passage three times.

What will you read for the first time? (accuracy)

What will you read for the second time? (expression)

What will you cross out each time you read? (a hippo)

The last time you read, use the timer. Read quickly, but accurately and with expression. See if you can finish reading before . . . one minute is up.

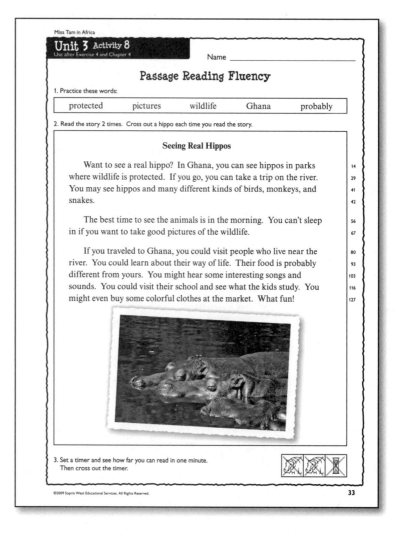

Miss Tam in Africa

Unit 3 Activity 8
Use after Exercise 4 and Chapter 4

Name _____

Passage Reading Fluency

1. Practice these words:

| protected | pictures | wildlife | Ghana | probably |

2. Read the story 2 times. Cross out a hippo each time you read the story.

Seeing Real Hippos

Want to see a real hippo? In Ghana, you can see hippos in parks where wildlife is protected. If you go, you can take a trip on the river. You may see hippos and many different kinds of birds, monkeys, and snakes. `14 29 41 42`

The best time to see the animals is in the morning. You can't sleep in if you want to take good pictures of the wildlife. `56 67`

If you traveled to Ghana, you could visit people who live near the river. You could learn about their way of life. Their food is probably different from yours. You might hear some interesting songs and sounds. You could visit their school and see what the kids study. You might even buy some colorful clothes at the market. What fun! `80 93 103 116 127`

3. Set a timer and see how far you can read in one minute. Then cross out the timer.

33

❶ SOUND REVIEW

Use selected Sound Cards from Units 1–3.

PACING

Exercise 5a should take about 10 minutes, allowing about 10 minutes for the Fact Summary Focus Lesson.

❷ ACCURACY AND FLUENCY BUILDING

- For each task, have students say any underlined part, then read the word.
- Set a pace. Then have students read the whole words in each task and column.
- Provide repeated practice, building accuracy first, then fluency. Mix group and individual turns.

C1. Multisyllabic Words

- For the list of words divided by syllables, have students read and finger count each syllable, then read the word. Use the word in a sentence, as appropriate.
- For the list of whole words, build accuracy and then fluency.

children	2 syllables	The bus was full of . . . *children*.
lessons	2 syllables	Candice works hard on her school . . . *lessons*.
important	3 syllables	Working hard in school is . . . *important*.
airport	2 syllables	We caught the plane at the . . . *airport*.
trickster	2 syllables	Someone who fools others is a . . . *trickster*.
Montgomery	3 syllables	Miss Tam lives in the city of . . . *Montgomery*.
respectfully	4 syllables	Jackson treats his grandparents . . . *respectfully*.
library	3 syllables	Pebo studies in the . . . *library*.
words	1 syllable	Do you know any Spanish . . . *words?*
animal	3 syllables	A giraffe is a very tall . . . *animal*.

D1. Tricky Words

- For each Tricky Word, have students identify known sounds or word parts. Use the word in a sentence to help with pronunciation.
- If the word is unfamiliar, tell students the word.

beautiful

Look at the first word. The first word part says /byoo/.
Say the word by parts with me. beau-ti-ful
The waterfall was . . . *beautiful*.
Read the word two times. (beautiful, beautiful)

Anansi (Uh-nan-see)

The next word is the name of an African story character. The word is *Anansi*.
Everyone say it. (Anansi) Some legends have a trickster spider in them called . . . *Anansi*.
Read the word three times. (Anansi, Anansi, Anansi)

weigh	I am five feet six inches tall. I wonder how many pounds I . . . *weigh*.
village	A small town in Ghana is called a . . . *village*.

❸ RHYMING WORDS

Have students read each set of words. Ask students how each set of words is the same.
How are the words the same? In the first box they all end with . . . *other*.

❹ MORPHOGRAPHS AND AFFIXES

❺ WORDS IN CONTEXT

Miss Tam in Africa

Unit 3 Exercise 5a
Use before Exercise 5b (Focus Lesson)

1. SOUND REVIEW Use selected Sound Cards from Units 1–3.

2. ACCURACY AND FLUENCY BUILDING For each column, have students say any underlined part, then read each word. Next, have students read the whole column.

A1 Mixed Practice	B1 Rhyming Words	C1 Multisyllabic Words		D1 Tricky Words
hard<u>l</u>y	b<u>ank</u>	chil·dren	children	beautiful
dr<u>u</u>mmers	th<u>ank</u>	les·sons	lessons	Anansi
wh<u>i</u>spered		im·por·tant	important	weigh
fl<u>ew</u>	bank<u>ed</u>	air·port	airport	village
wr<u>o</u>te	thank<u>ed</u>	trick·ster	trickster	library
t<u>a</u>le		Mont·gom·¢ry	Montgomery	words
sp<u>o</u>ke		res·pect·ful·ly	respectfully	animal

3. RHYMING WORDS Have students read each word set for accuracy, then fluency. Ask how the words are the same.

other	mother	another	rider	wider	spider

4. MORPHOGRAPHS AND AFFIXES Have students read the underlined word part, then the word.

tradi<u>tion</u>	<u>ex</u>plain	<u>re</u>turn	<u>un</u>do

5. WORDS IN CONTEXT Have students use the sounds and word parts they know and then the sentences to pronounce each underlined word.

A	daugh·ter	I have three children. Ana is my <u>daughter</u>.
B	h̷on·est	Bob does not cheat. He is very <u>honest</u>.
C	read	The woman liked the stories. She <u>read</u> them all.
D	learned	I went to the library. I <u>learned</u> how to look up books.
E	lis·t̷ened	Ben did what his dad told him to do. Ben <u>listened</u> to his dad.

21

MASTERY TEACHING/ DISCRIMINATION PRACTICE

Repeated Practice

Provide repeated practice on each task. If you hear an error, gently correct the whole group with a demonstration and/or guided practice. Move to another skill or task, then return to the difficult item many times—mixing group and individual turns, independent of your voice. When a task is easy, build speed of recognition.

Remember, practice makes perfect! And practice builds fluency.

FACT SUMMARY

COMPREHENSION PROCESSES
Remember, Understand, Analyze

⭐❶ **FACT SUMMARY INTRODUCTION**

Demonstrate and guide the process of writing a simple, three-fact summary. Students will not write in their books. They will respond orally and watch while you write.

• Introduce the Fact Summary Focus Lesson. Say something like:

Today, we're going to work on writing a fact summary. A fact summary is a strategy for remembering and understanding what you've read.

What is a fact? **(A fact is something that is real. A fact is true.)**

Yes, and a summary is a short version of something you've read or heard. So a fact summary is a shortened version of facts you've read about.

❷ **IDENTIFYING AND LOCATING FACTS**
Identifying—Facts; Locating Information

• Have students choral read the title and passage.
• Have students read Fact 1 and locate the information in the passage.

Now you are going to help me write a fact summary.

Fact 1 is already written for us. Read Fact 1.

(African elephants are the world's biggest land animals.)

Find the sentence in the passage that tells us this fact.

Everyone, read that fact. **(African elephants are the world's biggest land animals.)**

• Have students complete Facts 2 and 3 by locating information in the passage.

We need to finish Fact 2. What does it say? **(African elephants may weigh . . .)**

Find the sentence in the passage that will help us complete the fact.

Everyone, read that fact. **(An African elephant may weigh as much as twelve small cars.)**

What should I write to complete the fact? **(as much as twelve small cars)**

What should I do if I can't remember how to spell *twelve*? **(Look in the passage.)**

Write "as much as twelve small cars" to complete Fact 2.

• Repeat for Fact 3. Accept all reasonable responses.
• Have students read the three facts.

❸ **DRAWING CONCLUSIONS**
Drawing Conclusions, Explaining

• Tell students the facts will help them explain whether an elephant would make a good pet.

Now put your finger on the part that says "Question." Let's read that part together.

(Do you think an African elephant would make a good pet? Why or why not?)

Raise your hand if you can complete the first sentence. Who thinks an elephant would make a good pet? Now use the facts you helped me write to explain why you think an elephant would make a good pet. This will be our fact summary. **(I think an elephant would make a good pet because . . .)**

• Repeat for the next sentence.

⭐= New in this unit

Miss Tam in Africa

Unit 3 Exercise 5b (Focus Lesson)
Use after Exercise 5a and before Chapter 5

FOCUS LESSON Skills and Strategies

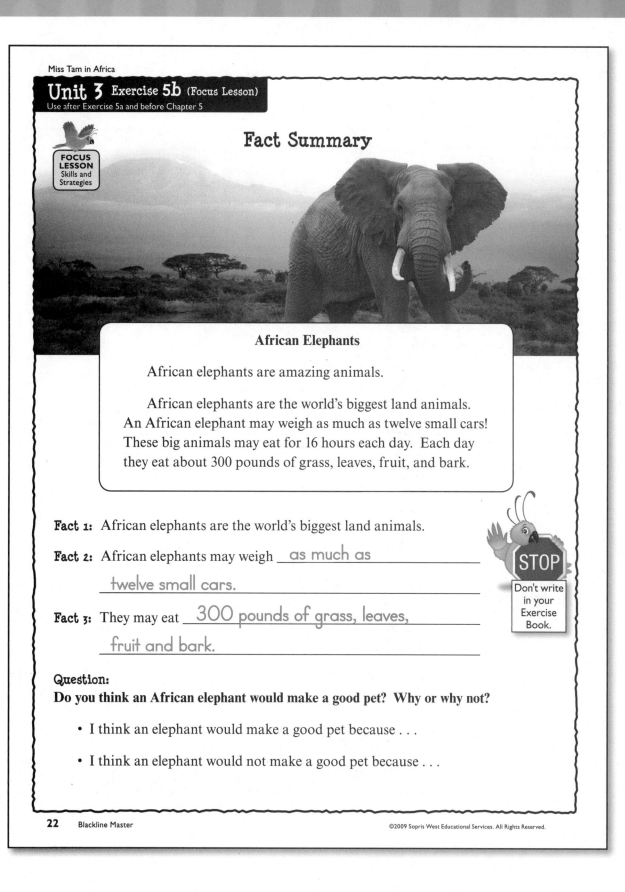

Fact Summary

African Elephants

African elephants are amazing animals.

African elephants are the world's biggest land animals. An African elephant may weigh as much as twelve small cars! These big animals may eat for 16 hours each day. Each day they eat about 300 pounds of grass, leaves, fruit, and bark.

Fact 1: African elephants are the world's biggest land animals.

Fact 2: African elephants may weigh _as much as_ _twelve small cars._

Fact 3: They may eat _300 pounds of grass, leaves,_ _fruit and bark._

STOP Don't write in your Exercise Book.

Question:

Do you think an African elephant would make a good pet? Why or why not?

- I think an elephant would make a good pet because . . .

- I think an elephant would not make a good pet because . . .

COMPREHENSION PROCESSES

Apply, Evaluate

PROCEDURES

Introducing Vocabulary

> ★trickster ★respect
> ★respectfully

- For each vocabulary word, have students read the word by parts, then read the whole word.
- Read the student-friendly explanations to students as they follow with their fingers. Then have students use the vocabulary word by following the gray text.
- Review and discuss the illustrations, as appropriate.

> **USING VOCABULARY**

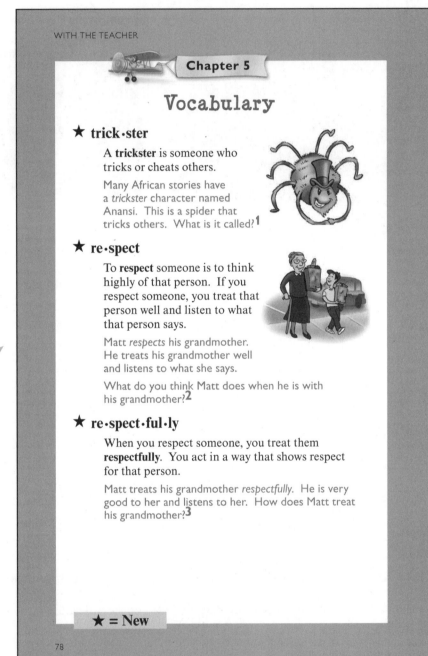

WITH THE TEACHER

Chapter 5

Vocabulary

★ **trick·ster**

A **trickster** is someone who tricks or cheats others.

Many African stories have a *trickster* character named Anansi. This is a spider that tricks others. What is it called?**1**

★ **re·spect**

To **respect** someone is to think highly of that person. If you respect someone, you treat that person well and listen to what that person says.

Matt *respects* his grandmother. He treats his grandmother well and listens to what she says.

What do you think Matt does when he is with his grandmother?**2**

★ **re·spect·ful·ly**

When you respect someone, you treat them **respectfully**. You act in a way that shows respect for that person.

Matt treats his grandmother *respectfully*. He is very good to her and listens to her. How does Matt treat his grandmother?**3**

★ = New

78

❶ Apply: Using Vocabulary—trickster (It's called a trickster.)

❷ Apply: Inferring; Making Connections; Using Vocabulary—respect (He shows respect by listening and doing what she tells him to do. He helps her do things like take out the trash . . .)

❸ Apply: Using Vocabulary—respectfully (Matt treats his grandmother respectfully.)

CHAPTER 5 INSTRUCTIONS

Students read with the teacher.

COMPREHENSION PROCESSES

Understand, Apply, Analyze, Evaluate

PROCEDURES

1. **Introducing Chapter 5**

   Reviewing; Identifying—Setting; Summarizing—Action; Using Vocabulary—Ghana, adventure; Predicting

   • Briefly review Chapters 1–4.

   Where is Miss Tam? (in Ghana)

   She is on an adventure. An adventure is doing something new and exciting.

   Why is Miss Tam's trip to Ghana an adventure?

   (She's never been to Ghana before, and it's an exciting adventure.)

   What did Miss Tam do in Ghana? (She went shopping, bargained for shoes, saw people in the market carrying things on their heads, and saw hippos.)

   • Explain that this is the end of the story. Ask students what they think will happen.

   This is the last chapter of "Miss Tam in Africa." What do you think will happen in this chapter?

2. **First Reading**

   • Ask questions and discuss the story as indicated by the gray text.

   • Mix group and individual turns, independent of your voice.
   Have students work toward a group accuracy goal of 0–4 errors.
   Quietly keep track of errors made by all students in the group.

   • After reading the story, practice any difficult words.
   Repeat if students have not reached the accuracy goal.

   > **CORRECTING DECODING ERRORS**
   >
   > During story reading, gently correct any error, then have students reread the sentence.

3. **Second Reading, Short Passage Practice: Developing Prosody**

   • Demonstrate expressive, fluent reading on the first paragraph. Read at a rate slightly faster than the students' rate. Say something like:

   Let's read the story again. Now that we know what it's about, we can really read it with expression. Listen to me read the first two paragraphs. I'm going to emphasize words I think are important.

   "*Soon* it was time to go back. Kwesi said they would stop in a village to listen to a storyteller. Miss Tam could *hardly wait* . . .

   • Guide practice with your voice.

   • Provide individual turns while others track with their fingers and whisper read.
   Provide descriptive, positive feedback.

   • Repeat with one paragraph or one page at a time.

4. **Partner Reading or Whisper Reading: Repeated Reading**

    Before beginning independent work, have students finger track and partner or whisper read.

5. **Homework 5: Repeated Reading**

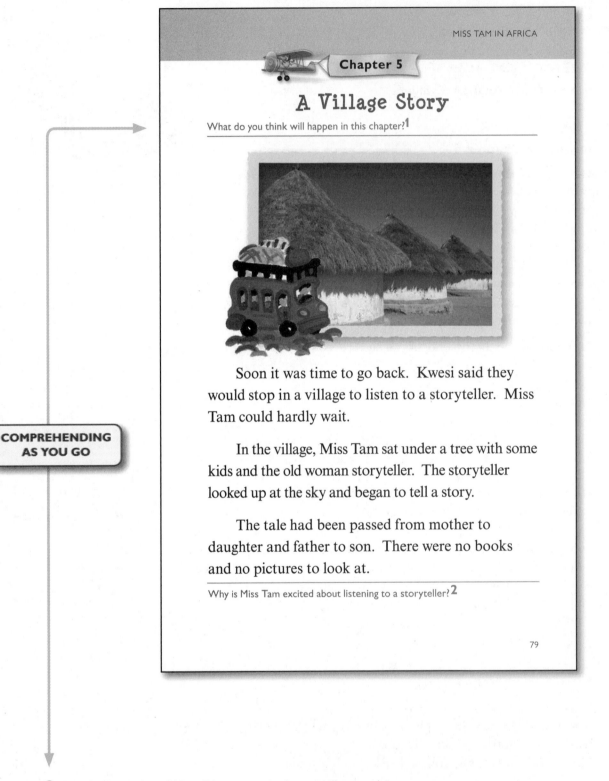

MISS TAM IN AFRICA

Chapter 5

A Village Story

What do you think will happen in this chapter?[1]

Soon it was time to go back. Kwesi said they would stop in a village to listen to a storyteller. Miss Tam could hardly wait.

In the village, Miss Tam sat under a tree with some kids and the old woman storyteller. The storyteller looked up at the sky and began to tell a story.

The tale had been passed from mother to daughter and father to son. There were no books and no pictures to look at.

Why is Miss Tam excited about listening to a storyteller?[2]

79

COMPREHENDING AS YOU GO

❶ **Apply:** Predicting (We will hear a story about a village . . .)

❷ **Apply:** Inferring, Explaining (Miss Tam has never listened to an African storyteller before. Miss Tam thinks the story will be very good. Miss Tam is a storyteller in Montgomery, so she likes hearing other storytellers.)

WITH THE TEACHER

As the old woman spoke, drummers played a different song for each animal and person in the story. Miss Tam listened carefully. The words and songs were beautiful.

Kwesi whispered, "The story is about a spider named Anansi." Miss Tam had read stories about this trickster to the children in Montgomery. Just like the children in Montgomery, the African children listened carefully and respectfully.

What is happening in the picture?**1** Why do you think Kwesi told Miss Tam what was happening in the story?**2**

80

COMPREHENDING AS YOU GO

❶ **Understand:** Explaining (The storyteller is telling a story to Miss Tam, Kwesi, and the children.)

❷ **Analyze:** Inferring; **Apply:** Explaining (Miss Tam doesn't understand what the storyteller is saying. The storyteller is speaking a different language . . .)

MISS TAM IN AFRICA

When the old woman was done, Kwesi said, "The storyteller asked the children what they learned from her story."

A small boy said, "It is important to be honest."

"It is important to work hard," another boy said.

A girl said, "It is important to respect others."

"Children learn important lessons from storytellers!" Kwesi said with a grin.

Describe what happens during storytelling in Ghana.**1** What did the children learn?**2** Look at the picture. How can you tell the children listened *respectfully*?**3**

81

MAKING CONNECTIONS
Lessons

After completing the page, briefly discuss how lessons taught in one country are often the same as in other countries. You may wish to say something like: The children in Ghana learned it was important to be honest. Is that important where we live? Why?

The children learned it was important to work hard. Is it important to work hard where we live? Why?

The children learned it is important to respect others. Is respecting others important where we live? Why?

COMPREHENDING AS YOU GO

1 **Understand:** Describing; Using Vocabulary—respectfully (Drummers play a song for each different person and animal. The children listen carefully and respectfully.)

2 **Understand:** Explaining—Lesson; Using Vocabulary—respect (The children learned that it is important to be honest, to work hard, and to respect others.)

3 **Apply:** Inferring (They are sitting quietly, paying attention to the storyteller . . .)

WITH THE TEACHER

Miss Tam's days in Ghana flew by. At the airport, Kwesi smiled and said, "I have a present for you. I wrote down the Anansi story so you can share it with the children in Montgomery."

With a tear in her eye, Miss Tam thanked Kwesi. While waiting for her plane, she sent an e-mail to her friends at the library.

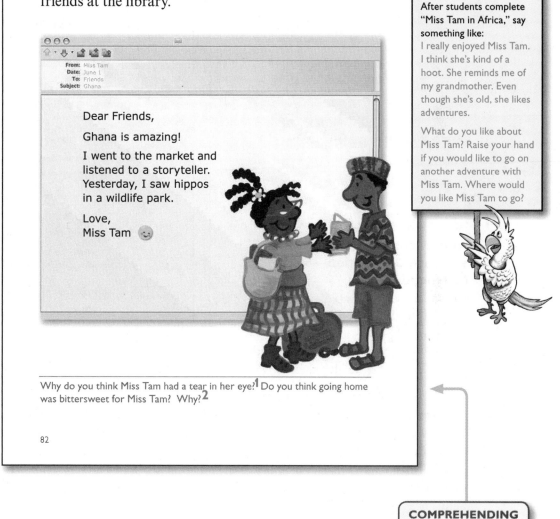

From: Miss Tam
Date: June 1
To: Friends
Subject: Ghana

Dear Friends,

Ghana is amazing!

I went to the market and listened to a storyteller. Yesterday, I saw hippos in a wildlife park.

Love,
Miss Tam

Why do you think Miss Tam had a tear in her eye?[1] Do you think going home was bittersweet for Miss Tam? Why?[2]

82

FOCUS ON RESPONDING

After students complete "Miss Tam in Africa," say something like:
I really enjoyed Miss Tam. I think she's kind of a hoot. She reminds me of my grandmother. Even though she's old, she likes adventures.

What do you like about Miss Tam? Raise your hand if you would like to go on another adventure with Miss Tam. Where would you like Miss Tam to go?

COMPREHENDING AS YOU GO

❶ **Apply:** Inferring, Explaining (Miss Tam had a tear in her eye because she is sad to say goodbye to Kwesi . . .)

❷ **Apply:** Inferring; Explaining; Using Vocabulary—Ghana (Yes, she is sad to leave Ghana but will be happy to go back home again . . .)

STORY MAP

COMPREHENSION PROCESSES

Remember, Understand, Apply

WRITING TRAITS

Conventions—Capital, Period

Using Graphic Organizer
Summarizing, Sequencing

Identifying—Setting

Describing—Character Traits
(Characterization)

Explaining—Beginning, Goal

Explaining—Middle, Action
Using Vocabulary—Ghana, bargain

Explaining—End, Outcome/Conclusion

PROCEDURES

**Story Map: Character Web,
Sentence Completion—Specific
Instructions**

- Have students complete the story
  map introduction. Say something like:
  A story map helps us remember
  important parts of the story. What's
  the first part? (the introduction)

  What are we going to tell about in the introduction? (the setting)
  Where did the story mostly happen? (in Africa)
  So what should we write in the box? (in Africa)
  We're also going to describe the main character, Miss Tam, in the introduction.
  What do we know about Miss Tam? (She's a librarian. She lives in Montgomery,
  Alabama. She's retired. She has pets . . .) Let's write "librarian" and "retired"
  and "has pets" on the lines.

- Repeat with the beginning.
- Guide students as they complete the middle.
  The middle of the story usually has a lot of action going on. We're going to read
  each sentence and fill in the blank to tell what happened in the middle. Read the
  first sentence . . .

- Guide students as they complete the end.
- After the story map is complete, have students read the story map.
  Ask them if it makes sense.

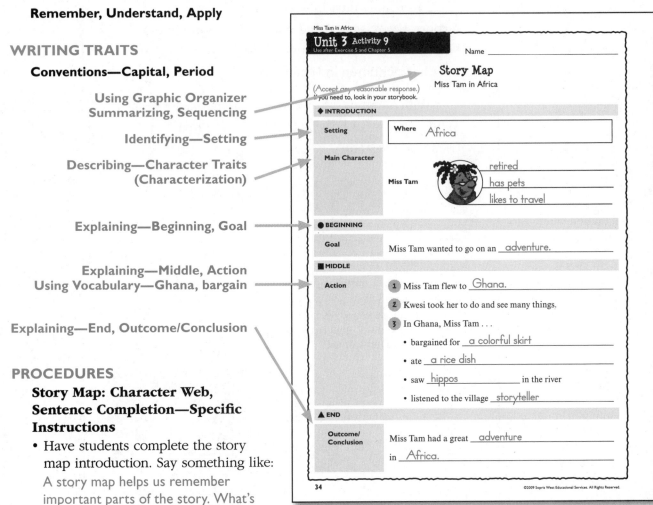

BUILDING
INDEPENDENCE

Using an overhead (BLM
copy) of the story map,
demonstrate and guide
how to complete each
section of the activity.

- For some groups,
  provide students with
  time to complete each
  section of their own
  story map before you
  demonstrate the next.

- For more independent
  writers, demonstrate
  and guide, then have
  students complete
  the story map
  independently.

STORY RETELL • SENTENCE JUMBLE

COMPREHENSION PROCESSES

Understand, Apply

WRITING TRAITS

Conventions—Complete Sentence, Beginning Capital, Period

Comprehension Monitoring Using Vocabulary—Africa, bargain, adventure, Ghana

---

Miss Tam in Africa

Unit 3 Activity 10
Use after Exercise 5 and Chapter 5

Name _____

Story Retell • Sentence Jumble
Miss Tam in Africa

Write the words in the correct order to make a sentence.

• went • Miss Tam • to Africa	Miss Tam went to Africa. _____
• bargained • she • for sandals	She bargained for sandals. _____
• saw hippos • in the river • Miss Tam	Miss Tam saw hippos in the river. _____
• listened • Miss Tam • to a storyteller	Miss Tam listened to a storyteller. _____
• a great adventure • she had • in Ghana	She had a great adventure in Ghana. _____

✓ Check and Correct

Do your sentences make sense?	☑
Do you have a capital at the beginning of each sentence and a period at the end?	☑

©2009 Sopris West Educational Services. All Rights Reserved.

35

PROCEDURES

For each step, demonstrate and guide practice, as needed. Then have students complete the page independently.

Sequencing Words: Story Retell—Specific Instructions

• Have students read the phrases in the boxes, identify who or what the sentence is about, and determine the word sequence. Say something like:

Read the words in the box.
(went, Miss Tam, to Africa)
Which words tell who the sentence is about? (Miss Tam)
So we might be able to start the sentence with "Miss Tam."
Now let's figure out the next part of the sentence.
Let's try "Miss Tam . . . went." That sounds okay.
Let's try "Miss Tam went to Africa." Does that sound right? (yes)

• Have students write the sentence. Remind them to start with a capital and end with a period.

So that's the sentence we'll write. I'm going to use my best handwriting. I'll write on the lines. I'm going to write small so everything fits on the line. What else? (You should start with a capital and end with a period.)

• Have students read the sentences they wrote, then determine if they make sense and retell the story.

When I finish writing the sentence, what should I do? (Read it.) That's right, you should read it to make sure it makes sense. What should you do if it doesn't make sense? (Try again.)

• Repeat with each sentence, as needed.

PURPOSE

Comprehension Monitoring

The Sentence Jumble is a simple activity, yet it provides important practice across multiple objectives.

• Students compose a complete sentence using the scaffold of words provided.

• Students learn an important self-monitoring strategy. They learn to ask "Does it make sense?" and to fix up work that doesn't.

• The end product also provides a model of a written retell.

1 SOUND REVIEW

Use selected Sound Cards from Units 1–3.

2 SHIFTY WORD BLENDING

For each word, have students say the underlined sound. Then have them sound out the word smoothly and say it. Use the words in sentences, as appropriate.

3 SOUND PRACTICE

- For each task, have students spell and say the focus sound in the gray bar.
- Next, have students read each underlined sound, the word, then the whole column.
- For the Bossy <u>E</u> Column, read the header, then have students identify whether the Bossy <u>E</u> is on the end of the word. Have students identify the underlined sound and then read the word.
- Repeat with each column, building accuracy first, then fluency.

4 ACCURACY AND FLUENCY BUILDING

A2. Compound Words

- Remind students that compound words are made when two words are joined.
- Have students read each small word and then the compound word.

C1. Multisyllabic Words

For each word, have students read each syllable, finger count, then read the word. Use the word in a sentence, as appropriate.

inches	2 syllables	One foot is equal to 12 . . . *inches.*
bottom	2 syllables	The penny sank to the . . . *bottom* . . . of the glass.
herbivore	3 syllables	An animal that eats mostly plants is an . . . *herbivore.*
during	2 syllables	The dogs hid under the shed . . . *during* . . . the storm.
probably	3 syllables	Meg wants to go to the park, so she will . . . *probably* go.
hippopotamus	5 syllables	Jaime went to the zoo and saw a . . . *hippopotamus.*

> **ACCURACY AND FLUENCY BUILDING (Reminder)**
> - For each task, have students say any underlined part, then read the word.
> - Set a pace. Then have students read the whole words in each task and column.
> - Provide repeated practice, building accuracy first, then fluency.

D1. Tricky Words

- For each Tricky Word, have students identify known sounds or word parts. Use the word in a sentence to help with pronunciation.
- If the word is unfamiliar, tell students the word. Then have students say, spell, and say it.

though

The first word is *though.* Say the word. (though)

Miss Tam understood the storyteller, even . . . *though* . . . she didn't speak the language.

Spell *though.* (<u>t-h-o-u-g-h</u>)

Say the word three times. (though, though, though)

weighs	My dog is very big. I wonder how much he . . . *weighs.*
southern	The state of Mississippi is in the . . . *southern* . . . United States.
curtain	The magician came out from behind the . . . *curtain.*

⑤ WORDS IN CONTEXT

- Tell students to use the sounds and word parts they know and then the sentence to figure out how to say each word. Assist, as needed.
- Have students read each word part, the whole word, and then the sentence.

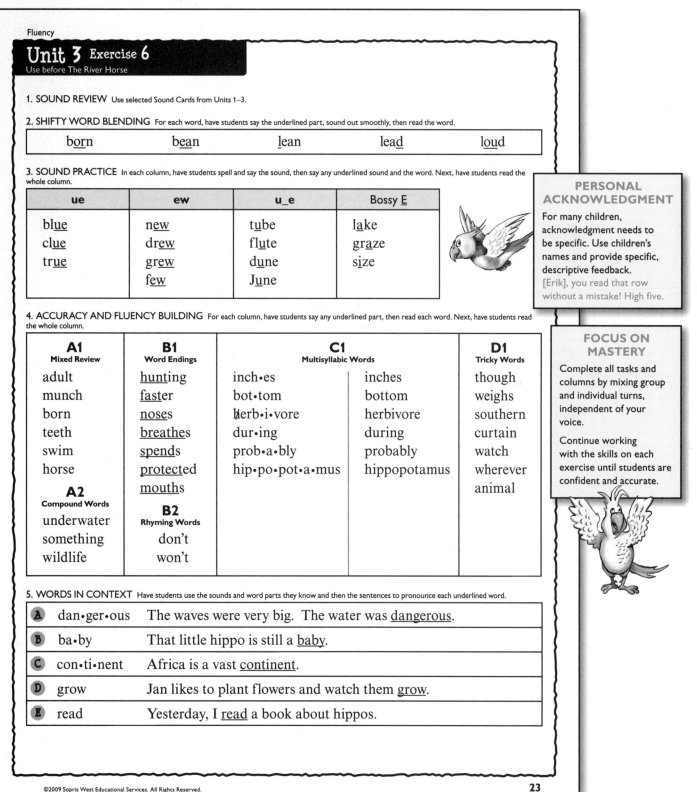

Fluency

Unit 3 Exercise 6
Use before The River Horse

1. SOUND REVIEW Use selected Sound Cards from Units 1–3.

2. SHIFTY WORD BLENDING For each word, have students say the underlined part, sound out smoothly, then read the word.

b<u>or</u>n	b<u>ea</u>n	<u>l</u>ean	lea<u>d</u>	l<u>ou</u>d

3. SOUND PRACTICE In each column, have students spell and say the sound, then say any underlined sound and the word. Next, have students read the whole column.

ue	ew	u_e	Bossy <u>E</u>
bl<u>ue</u>	n<u>ew</u>	t<u>u</u>b<u>e</u>	l<u>a</u>ke
cl<u>ue</u>	dr<u>ew</u>	fl<u>u</u>te	gr<u>a</u>ze
tr<u>ue</u>	grew	d<u>u</u>ne	s<u>i</u>ze
	f<u>ew</u>	June	

PERSONAL ACKNOWLEDGMENT

For many children, acknowledgment needs to be specific. Use children's names and provide specific, descriptive feedback. [Erik], you read that row without a mistake! High five.

4. ACCURACY AND FLUENCY BUILDING For each column, have students say any underlined part, then read each word. Next, have students read the whole column.

A1 Mixed Review	B1 Word Endings	C1 Multisyllabic Words		D1 Tricky Words
adult	<u>hunting</u>	inch•es	inches	though
munch	<u>faster</u>	bot•tom	bottom	weighs
born	<u>noses</u>	<u>h</u>erb•i•vore	herbivore	southern
teeth	<u>breathes</u>	dur•ing	during	curtain
swim	<u>spends</u>	prob•a•bly	probably	watch
horse	<u>protected</u>	hip•po•pot•a•mus	hippopotamus	wherever
A2 Compound Words	<u>mouths</u>			animal
underwater	**B2** Rhyming Words			
something	don't			
wildlife	won't			

FOCUS ON MASTERY

Complete all tasks and columns by mixing group and individual turns, independent of your voice.

Continue working with the skills on each exercise until students are confident and accurate.

5. WORDS IN CONTEXT Have students use the sounds and word parts they know and then the sentences to pronounce each underlined word.

Ⓐ	dan•ger•ous	The waves were very big. The water was <u>dangerous</u>.
Ⓑ	ba•by	That little hippo is still a <u>baby</u>.
Ⓒ	con•ti•nent	Africa is a vast <u>continent</u>.
Ⓓ	grow	Jan likes to plant flowers and watch them <u>grow</u>.
Ⓔ	read	Yesterday, I <u>read</u> a book about hippos.

23

COMPREHENSION PROCESSES

Remember, Understand, Apply

PROCEDURES

1. Reviewing the Table of Contents

Using Table of Contents; Identifying—Title

Have students use the Table of Contents on page 5 of their storybooks to find the title page for "The River Horse."

Put your finger on the title of our next story. What's the title of our next story? (The River Horse)

What page should we turn to find our next story? (page 83)

2. Introducing the Story

Identifying—Title, Author

- Have students turn to page 83 and identify the story title and author.
  "The River Horse" is an interesting title. What's the title?
  (The River Horse)
  Who is the author? (Paula Rich)
- Discuss the gray text questions under the picture.

TABLE OF CONTENTS

UNIT 3 • African Adventures

5

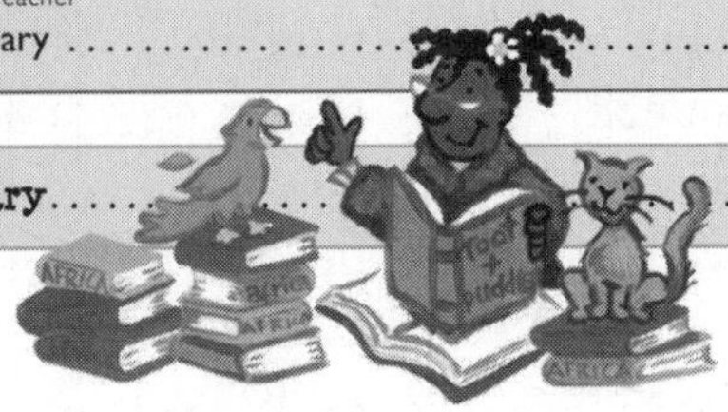

The River Horse
by Paula Rich

What do you see in the picture?**1** Where do you think this story takes place?**2**

83

COMPREHENDING
AS YOU GO

1 Understand: Explaining (I see water. I see lumps in the water. I see trees. I think I see hippos.)

2 Apply: Inferring—Where; Using Vocabulary—Africa (I think it takes place in Africa.)

COMPREHENSION PROCESSES

Understand, Apply

PROCEDURES

Introducing Vocabulary

> ★amazing, continent
> ★herbivore ★graze

- For each vocabulary word, have students read the word by parts, then read the whole word.
- Read the student-friendly explanations to students as they follow with their fingers. Then have students use the vocabulary word by following the gray text.
- Review and discuss the photos and illustrations, as appropriate.

USING VOCABULARY

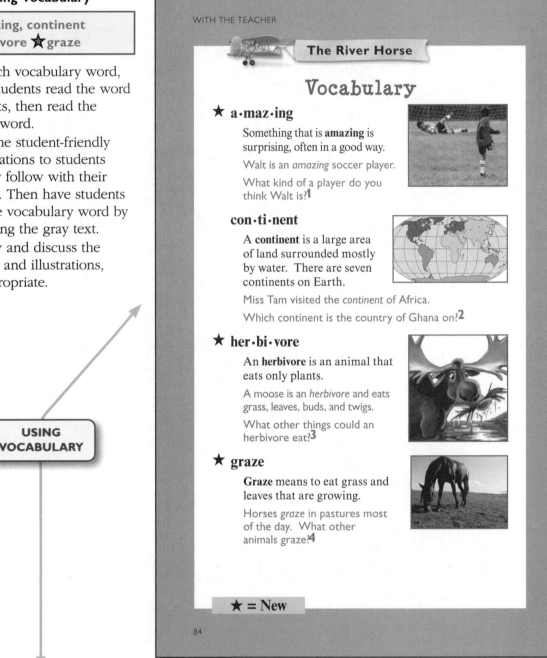

WITH THE TEACHER

The River Horse

Vocabulary

★ **a·maz·ing**

Something that is **amazing** is surprising, often in a good way.

Walt is an *amazing* soccer player.

What kind of a player do you think Walt is?**1**

con·ti·nent

A **continent** is a large area of land surrounded mostly by water. There are seven continents on Earth.

Miss Tam visited the *continent* of Africa.

Which continent is the country of Ghana on?**2**

★ **her·bi·vore**

An **herbivore** is an animal that eats only plants.

A moose is an *herbivore* and eats grass, leaves, buds, and twigs.

What other things could an herbivore eat?**3**

★ **graze**

Graze means to eat grass and leaves that are growing.

Horses *graze* in pastures most of the day. What other animals graze?**4**

★ = New

84

❶ **Understand:** Defining Vocabulary—amazing (Walt is a surprisingly good soccer player.)

❷ **Apply:** Inferring; Using Vocabulary—Ghana, continent, Africa (Ghana is on the continent of Africa.)

❸ **Apply:** Inferring; Using Vocabulary—herbivore (An herbivore could eat flowers, berries, bushes . . .)

❹ **Apply:** Priming Background Knowledge; Using Vocabulary—graze (Other animals that graze are cows, goats, sheep . . .)

STORY READING INSTRUCTIONS
Students read with the teacher.

COMPREHENSION PROCESSES
Remember, Understand, Apply, Analyze

PROCEDURES

1. Introducing "The River Horse"

Inferring, Explaining
- "The River Horse" starts with a riddle. Say something like:
  What does it say at the top of page 85?
  (There is something behind the curtain. What could it be?)
  What fun. We're going to be working on a riddle.
  What do you think is behind the curtain? (an animal)

2. Reading the Riddle, pages 85 and 86
- After each clue, ask students what they think is behind the curtain.
  After Clue 1 and student responses, say something like:
  Some of you think it might be a hippo. Some of you think it might be an elephant.
  Why don't you think it's a mouse? (It's as big as a car.)
  Repeat with Clues 2–4.
- Have students turn to page 86 to find out the answer.

3. First Reading, pages 86–89
- Ask questions and discuss the story, as indicated by the gray text.
- Mix group and individual turns, independent of your voice.
  Have students work toward a group accuracy goal of 0–3 errors.
  Quietly keep track of errors made by all students in the group.
- After reading the story, practice any difficult words. Reread the story if students have not reached the accuracy goal.

4. Second Reading, Short Passage Practice: Developing Prosody
- Demonstrate expressive, fluent reading of the first two paragraphs.
- Guide practice with your voice.
- Provide individual turns while others track with their fingers and whisper read.
- Repeat with one paragraph or page at a time.
  Listen to my expression as I read the first page. I'm going to read like a TV moderator on a science show. I'm going to emphasize information that I think is interesting.
  "A Hippo's Size: *Hippopotamus* is a big word that means river horse. Hippos are much bigger than . . . "
- Guide practice with your voice.
  Read the first page with me—as if you were a TV moderator.

5. Partner Reading or Whisper Reading: Repeated Reading
 Before beginning independent work, have students finger track and partner or whisper read.

6. Homework 6: Repeated Reading

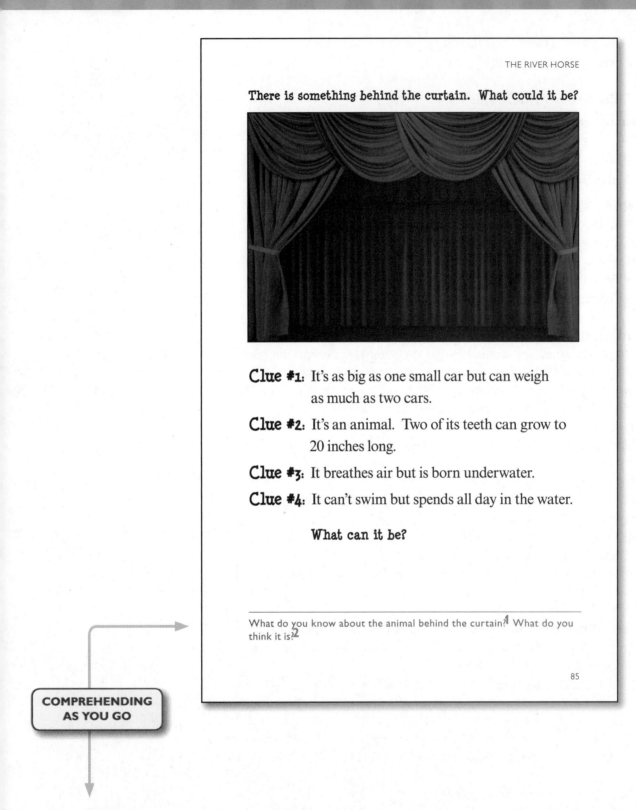

THE RIVER HORSE

There is something behind the curtain. What could it be?

Clue #1: It's as big as one small car but can weigh as much as two cars.

Clue #2: It's an animal. Two of its teeth can grow to 20 inches long.

Clue #3: It breathes air but is born underwater.

Clue #4: It can't swim but spends all day in the water.

What can it be?

What do you know about the animal behind the curtain?[1] What do you think it is?[2]

85

COMPREHENDING AS YOU GO

① **Understand:** Summarizing (It's very big. It's an animal. It breathes air but is born underwater. It spends the day in the water but can't swim . . .)

② **Analyze:** Inferring (A hippo; an elephant; a polar bear . . .)

WITH THE TEACHER

What animal is this?

The amazing hippopotamus!

A Hippo's Size

Hippopotamus is a big word that means river horse. Hippos are much bigger than horses though. They are only four to five feet tall, but they can weigh more than your family's car!

What does *hippopotamus* mean?[1] Why is that a good name?[2]

86

COMPREHENDING AS YOU GO

❶ **Remember:** Identifying—What (Hippopotamus means river horse.)

❷ **Apply:** Inferring, Explaining (It is a good name because a hippo is an animal like a horse but lives in the river.)

THE RIVER HORSE

A Hippo's Habitat

Hippos live in Africa. They used to live all over the southern part of the continent. They lived wherever there was a river or lake and grass to eat. Now there are not so many hippos. They live mostly in wildlife parks, where they are protected from hunting.

Hippos live where it is hot. They spend all day in the water to keep cool. Often only the tips of their noses, ears, and eyes stick out of the water.

FOCUS ON VOCABULARY— habitat
After reading the heading, define the word "habitat." Say something like: *Habitat* is a snazzy word for the natural home or place an animal lives. What's another word for the natural place an animal lives? (habitat)

LOCATING INFORMATION
Previewing, Using Headings, Predicting
What do you think you're going to learn about in this section? (the hippo's habitat, where it lives . . .)

Describe a hippo's habitat?[1] Why are they mostly found in *wildlife* parks now?[2]

87

COMPREHENDING AS YOU GO

❶ **Remember:** Describing; Using Vocabulary—Africa, habitat (A hippo's habitat is in Africa. They live near rivers and lakes. They live where it is hot.)

❷ **Understand:** Explaining; Using Vocabulary—wildlife (Hippos are mostly found in wildlife parks because there they are protected from hunting.)

WITH THE TEACHER

A Hippo's Food

During the day, adult hippos walk on the river bottom and munch on underwater plants.

At night, hippos leave the water and graze on grass near the river. Hippos do not eat meat. They eat plants. Hippos are herbivores.

Adult hippos walk on the river bottom. Only baby hippos can swim.

Where do hippos eat?**1** What do hippos eat?**2** What makes a hippo an herbivore?**3**

88

COMPREHENDING AS YOU GO

1 **Remember:** Identifying—Facts (Hippos eat in the river during the day. At night, they eat near the river.)

2 **Remember:** Identifying—Facts (Hippos eat underwater plants and grass.)

3 **Understand:** Explaining; Using Vocabulary—herbivore (Hippos are herbivores because they eat only plants.)

THE RIVER HORSE

Watch Out!

Hippos are dangerous animals. They have long sharp teeth and big mouths. You could probably stand in a hippo's mouth when it's wide open! Hippos run faster than most people, so watch out. Don't get too close to a hippo!

A hippo's two biggest teeth may grow to be 20 inches long.

Why is it important to stay away from hippos? [1] You've learned many facts about hippos. What makes them *amazing* animals? [2]

89

COMPREHENDING AS YOU GO

❶ **Understand:** Explaining (Hippos are dangerous, so it is important to stay away from them. They have long sharp teeth and can run faster than most people.)

❷ **Apply:** Summarizing—Facts; Using Vocabulary—amazing (Hippos are amazing because they can walk underwater. Hippos are amazing because they are really big. Hippos are amazing because they weigh as much as two cars . . .)

PASSAGE COMPREHENSION

COMPREHENSION PROCESSES
Remember, Understand, Apply

WRITING TRAITS
Conventions—Complete Sentence, Capital, Period

Identifying—Topic

Identifying—What

Locating Information
Identifying—Topics, Headings

Identifying—Facts

Identifying—Fact
Using Vocabulary—Africa, protected

Inferring

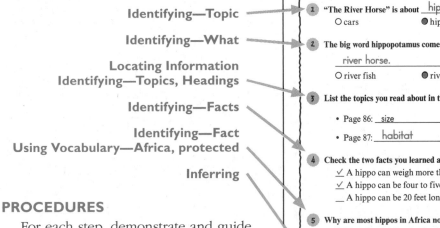

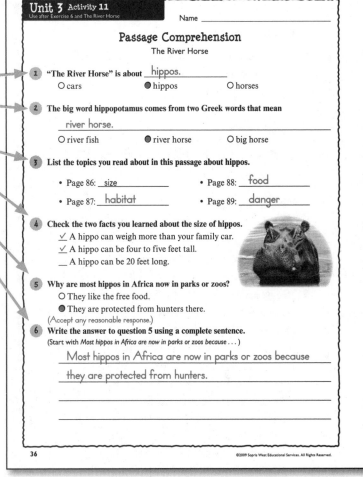

The River Horse

Unit 3 Activity 11
Use after Exercise 6 and The River Horse

Name _____

Passage Comprehension
The River Horse

1. "The River Horse" is about ___hippos.___
   ○ cars   ● hippos   ○ horses

2. The big word hippopotamus comes from two Greek words that mean
   ___river horse.___
   ○ river fish   ● river horse   ○ big horse

3. List the topics you read about in this passage about hippos.
   - Page 86: ___size___   - Page 88: ___food___
   - Page 87: ___habitat___   - Page 89: ___danger___

4. Check the two facts you learned about the size of hippos.
   ✓ A hippo can weigh more than your family car.
   ✓ A hippo can be four to five feet tall.
   __ A hippo can be 20 feet long.

5. Why are most hippos in Africa now in parks or zoos?
   ○ They like the free food.
   ● They are protected from hunters there.
   (Accept any reasonable response.)

6. Write the answer to question 5 using a complete sentence.
   (Start with *Most hippos in Africa are now in parks or zoos because . . .*)
   ___Most hippos in Africa are now in parks or zoos because___
   ___they are protected from hunters.___

36

©2009 Sopris West Educational Services. All Rights Reserved.

PROCEDURES

For each step, demonstrate and guide practice, as needed. Then have students complete the page independently.

1. **Selection Response—Basic Instructions** (Items 1, 2, 4, 5)
   Have students read each question or sentence, then fill in the bubble and/or blank with the correct answer or check the correct items. Remind students to put a period at the end of sentences.

2. **Making Lists—Specific Instructions** (Item 3)
   - Have students read the instruction and list the topics. Remind them to look back in their storybooks. Say something like:
     You're going to look in your book to list the topics. The topic, or what the section is about, is often in the headings.
     Look on page 86. Touch the heading. That tells you what the section is about. What is the topic? (A Hippo's Size) Yes, so you're going to learn about the size of the hippo. So you'll write "size" after "Page 86."

   - Repeat with remaining topics as needed.

3. **Sentence Writing—Basic Instructions** (Item 6)
   Have students read the instruction and write a complete sentence response using the information from Item 5. Have students read the starting phrase. Remind them to start with a capital and end with a period.

   Self-monitoring
   Have students check and correct their work.

★FACT SUMMARY

COMPREHENSION PROCESSES
Remember, Understand, Apply, Analyze, Evaluate, Create

WRITING TRAITS
Conventions—Complete Sentence, Capital, Period

Identifying—Facts

Inferring, Explaining, Drawing Conclusions, Making Judgments, Generating Ideas

PROCEDURES
For each step, demonstrate and guide practice, as needed. Then have students complete the page independently.

1. Sentence Copying, Sentence Completion—Specific Instructions (Item 1)

- Have students read the main idea.
- Tell students they are going to write four facts that tell why hippos are amazing animals. Have students read Fact 1 and tell them that they will copy that fact on the lines. Repeat with Fact 2.
- Have students read the beginning of Fact 3 and orally complete the sentence. Have students write their answers in the blank. Remind them that they can look in their storybooks.
- For Fact 4, have students orally identify another fact that explains why hippos are amazing animals. Remind students to use the sentence starter in the parentheses to write a good sentence.

2. Personal Response: Sentence Completion—Specific Instructions (Item 2)

Have students fill in the blank by using facts that support their opinion. Say something like:
We need to figure out whether a hippo would make a good pet.
Thumbs up if you think hippos would not make a good pet.
I agree with you, so I'm going to use a fact to explain why.
I think a hippo would not make a good pet because they spend most of their time in rivers.
I don't have a river near my home, so a hippo would be unhappy at my house.
Tell me why you think a hippo would not make a good pet.
Start with the sentence starter and be sure to use a fact. (I think a hippo would not make a good pet because . . .)

The River Horse

Unit 3 Activity 12
Use after Exercise 6 and The River Horse

Name _____

★Fact Summary
The River Horse

1 **Main Idea: Hippos are amazing animals.**
Write 4 facts that tell why hippos are amazing animals. You may wish to look in your storybook.

- **Copy fact 1:** Hippos can weigh as much as two cars.
  Hippos can weigh as much as two cars.
  _____

- **Copy fact 2:** They are born underwater.
  They are born underwater.
  _____

- **Complete fact 3:** They spend all day in __the water.__
  (Accept any reasonable response.)
- **Write your own fact 4.**
  Use a complete sentence. (Start with *Hippos* . . .)
  Hippos can be dangerous, so watch out.
  _____

(Accept any reasonable response.)
2 **Do you think a hippo would make a good pet? Why or why not?**
Use at least one fact about hippos in your answer.

I think a hippo __would not__ make a good pet because . . .
          would   (would not)

they are too big and would eat too much.
_____
_____

©2009 Sopris West Educational Services. All Rights Reserved.   37

★ = New in this unit

JUST FOR FUN • MAKE A POSTCARD FOR MISS TAM

Miss Tam in Africa

Unit 3 Just for Fun
Use as appropriate

Name _____

Just for Fun • Make a Postcard for Miss Tam

1 Draw a picture on the front of the postcard.

2 Write a note to Miss Tam.

Dear Miss Tam,
  I think it is cool
  that you went to
  Ghana. Come to
  Colorado. We have
  mountains.
Yours truly, Greg

Miss Tam
85 Read Well Street
Montgomery, Alabama
12345

38   ©2009 Sopris West Educational Services. All Rights Reserved.

HOW TO USE "JUST FOR FUN" ACTIVITIES

Note: This activity is optional and is *just for fun.*
Use the activity:
• as a cushion activity
• for homework
• just for fun

PROCEDURES

For each step, demonstrate and guide practice, as needed. Then have students complete the page independently. Tell students they will make and write a postcard to Miss Tam. Have students illustrate the postcard with a scene from their neighborhood. Then have students write a note to Miss Tam.

1. **Illustrating—Specific Instructions** (Item 1)

   Have students read the sentence. Have students brainstorm ideas about what they could draw for a picture that represents their neighborhood. Have students visualize and draw a picture.

2. **Sentence Writing—Specific Instructions** (Item 2)

   Have students read the "Dear Miss Tam" and then brainstorm what they would like to say to Miss Tam. Have students write a note to Miss Tam using complete sentences. Remind students to begin with a capital and put a period at the end.

Note: Miss Tam and her address are fictional. You may wish to intercede for Miss Tam and write back to the children.

End of the Unit

In this section, you will find:

Making Decisions

As you near the end of the unit, plan to give the Oral Reading Fluency Assessment to each child in your group.

Oral Reading Fluency Assessment

The Unit 3 Oral Reading Fluency Assessment is located on page 86 of this teacher's guide and in the *Assessment Manual*.

Certificate of Achievement and Goal Setting

Celebrate your children's accomplishments. When your students master the unit skills, send home the Certificate of Achievement. Have students set goals for the next unit.

Extra Practice Lessons

Use the Extra Practice lessons for students who need additional decoding and fluency work. Student materials can be copied from the Extra Practice blackline masters.

Making Decisions

USING THE ORAL READING FLUENCY RESULTS

At the end of each unit, you will need to make decisions regarding student progress. Should students go forward in the program? Does the group need Extra Practice before proceeding? Do individuals require more assistance and practice to continue working in their group? These decisions all require use of the oral reading fluency data and professional judgment. As you analyze assessment results, watch for trends and anomalies. See the *Assessment Manual* for detailed information and instructional recommendations. General guidelines and recommendations follow:

Strong Pass ≥ 102 WCPM 0–2 errors	• Continue with the current pace of instruction. • Have students set goals. (Until students are reading approximately 180 words correct per minute, oral reading fluency continues to be an instructional goal.)
Pass 81–101 WCPM 0–2 errors	• Continue with the current pace of instruction. Consider increasing fluency practice.
No Pass ≤ 80 WCPM	If a child scores a No Pass but has previously passed all assessments, you may wish to advance the student to the next unit: • Carefully monitor student performance and/or • Provide additional practice opportunities. (See below.) If a child scores two consecutive No Passes or periodic No Passes, additional practice must be provided. (See below.) If a child scores three consecutive No Passes, the student needs intervention immediately. • Retest for placement in a lower-performing group. • Provide a double dose of instruction. (See below.)

RED FLAG
A No Pass is a red flag. A mild early intervention can prevent an intense and time-consuming intervention in the future.

Added Practice Options for Groups

Warm-Ups: Begin each Story Reading with a review of the previous day's story.

Extended Units: If several children begin to score No Passes or barely pass, consider extending the unit by adding Extra Practice 1, 2, and/or 3. Extra Practice lessons.

Vowel Review: Consider a review of selected vowel units from *RW1* or *RW2 FF*.

Added Practice Options for Individual Students

Tutorials: Set up five-minute tutorials on a daily basis. Use Extra Practice lessons.

Double Dose: Find ways to provide a double dose of *Read Well* instruction.

END-OF-THE-UNIT CELEBRATION

When students pass, celebrate with the Certificate of Achievement.

Note: Using the Flesch-Kincaid Grade Level readability formula, the Unit 3 Assessment has a 2.2 readability level.

GOAL SETTING (*optional*)

Goal Setting

I've improved my reading by __3__ words correct per minute.
My new goal is to read __86__ words correct per minute.
I will work on my goal by:
• Reading and rereading carefully
• Working hard in reading group
• *Finger tracking*

Signed __Amber__
Date __Sept. 28__

How I Did:
My fluency was __84__
Goal Met ___ Exceeded: ✓

TRICKY WORD and FOCUS SKILL WARM-UP

through	learned	adventure	cute	wade	beautiful

ORAL READING FLUENCY PASSAGE

Miss Tam's African Adventure

★Miss Tam went on a great trip to Africa. It was an amazing adventure. In Africa, Miss Tam learned many new customs. — 12 / 21 / 22

Miss Tam went on a river trip. She saw monkeys, hippos, and beautiful birds. — 33 / 36

The monkeys were a lot of fun. Miss Tam saw cute little monkeys eating leaves in the trees. — 48 / 54

The hippos were awesome. Miss Tam saw the hippos near the river. She saw them wade through the mud and then eat the green grass. — 63 / 76 / 79

The birds were colorful. They were red, blue, green, and black. A small bird flew by, but then it landed near Miss Tam. The bird made Miss Tam think about Minnie Bird. — 89 / 102 / 111

Miss Tam would be happy to go back home. She missed her pets, but she had a grand time in Africa. — 122 / 132

ORAL READING FLUENCY	Start timing at the ★. Mark errors. Make a single slash in the text (/) at 60 seconds. Have the student complete the passage. If the student completes the passage in less than 60 seconds, have the student go back to the ★ and continue reading. Make a double slash in the text (//) at 60 seconds.
WCPM	Determine words correct per minute by subtracting errors from words read in 60 seconds.
STRONG PASS	The student scores no more than 2 errors on the first pass through the passage and reads 102 or more words correct per minute. Proceed to Unit 4 or 5.
PASS	The student scores no more than 2 errors on the first pass through the passage and reads 81 to 101 words correct per minute. Proceed to Unit 4 or 5.
NO PASS	The student scores 3 or more errors on the first pass through the passage and/or reads 80 or fewer words correct per minute. Provide added fluency practice with RW2 Unit 3 Extra Practice. (Lessons follow the certificate at the end of the teacher's guide.) After completing the Extra Practice, retest the student.

Amazing Achievement

_____

has successfully completed

Read Well 2 Unit 3 · African Adventures

with _____ words correct per minute.

Teacher Signature _____

Date _____

- -

Goal Setting

I've improved my reading by _____ words correct per minute.

My new goal is to read _____ words correct per minute.

I will work on my goal by:

- Reading and rereading carefully
- Working hard in reading group
- _____

Signed _____

Date _____

How I Did:

My fluency was _____

Goal: Met _____ Exceeded: _____

PROCEDURES

1. Sound Review

Use selected Sound Cards from Units 1–3.
- Have students say each sound, building accuracy first, then fluency.
- Mix group and individual turns, independent of your voice.

2. Sounding Out Smoothly
- For each word, have students say the underlined part, sound out the word smoothly, then read the whole word. (Use the words in sentences, as needed.)
- Have students read all the words in the row, building accuracy first, then fluency.
- Repeat practice. Mix group and individual turns, independent of your voice.

3. Accuracy and Fluency Building
- For each task, have students say any underlined part, then read each word.
- Set a pace. Then have students read the whole words in each task and column.
- Provide repeated practice, building accuracy first, then fluency.

4. Tricky Words

Have students read each row for accuracy, then fluency.

5. Multisyllabic Words

For each word, have students read each syllable out loud, finger count the syllables, then tell how many syllables are in the word. If needed, use the word in a sentence. Have students read the whole word.

6. Dictation

arm, art, part, tight, right, might
- Say "arm." Have students say the word. Guide students as they finger count and say the sounds. Have students touch or write the sounds, then read the word. Say something like:

   The first word is **arm.** Say the word. (arm)

   Say and count the sounds in **arm** with me.

   Hold up one finger for each sound. /ar/•/mmm/ How many sounds? (two)

   What's the first sound? (/ar/) What letter pattern makes the /ar/ sound? (a-r) Write /ar/.

   What's the last sound? (/mmm/) Touch under /mmm/.

   Read the word. (arm)

- Repeat with "art" and "part."
- Continue with the rhyming words: tight, right, might.

Unit 3 Decoding Practice

Name _____

1. SOUND REVIEW Use selected Sound Cards from Units 1–3.

2. SOUNDING OUT SMOOTHLY Have students say the underlined part, sound out and read each word, then read the row.

dr<u>u</u>m	l<u>a</u>st	h<u>e</u>ld	sk<u>i</u>ns

3. ACCURACY/FLUENCY BUILDING Have students say any underlined part, then read each word. Next, have students read the column.

A1 Sound Practice	**B1** Word Endings	**C1** Rhyming Words	**D1** Compound Words
n<u>ew</u>	amaze	th<u>ough</u>t	inside
gr<u>ew</u>	amazing	b<u>ough</u>t	outside
fl<u>ew</u>		br<u>ough</u>t	without
	story		
A2 Mixed Practice	stories	**C2** Bossy E	**D2** Mixed Review
bl<u>ue</u>	**B2** Sound Practice	m<u>a</u>d<u>e</u>	deep
s<u>aw</u>	<u>al</u>so	lik<u>e</u>	sharp
s<u>ou</u>nd	<u>al</u>ways	tim<u>e</u>	wood
squ<u>ee</u>ze	<u>al</u>most	th<u>e</u>s<u>e</u>	more
pl<u>ay</u>		c<u>u</u>t<u>e</u>	away

4. TRICKY WORDS Have students read each row for accuracy, then fluency.

Ⓐ	talking	animal	covered	music	people	5
Ⓑ	beautiful	two	again	others	colorful	10

5. MULTISYLLABIC WORDS Have students read the word by parts, tell how many syllables are in the word, then read the whole word.

Ⓐ	awe•some	awesome	lit•tle	little
Ⓑ	un•der	under	Chap•man	Chapman
Ⓒ	Af•ri•can	African	ad•ven•ture	adventure

6. DICTATION Say the word. Have students say the word, then finger count and say the sounds. Have students say each sound as they touch or write it.

A1 Shifty Words	**B1** Rhyming Words
<u>a</u> r m	t <u>igh</u>t
ar <u>t</u>	r <u>igh</u>t
<u>p</u> ar t	m <u>igh</u>t

19

PROCEDURES

1. First Reading

Mix group and individual turns, independent of your voice. Have students work toward an accuracy goal of 0–2 errors and practice any difficult words.

2. Second Reading, Short Passage Practice: Developing Prosody

• Demonstrate how to read a line or two with expression. Read at a rate slightly faster than the students' rate. Say something like: Listen as I read the first two sentences with expression and phrasing. I'm going to emphasize certain words and pause between sentences.

"One day last year, Mr. Chapman brought a cool drum to class. It was made of wood."

• Guide practice with your voice. Now read the paragraph with me.

• Provide individual turns while others track with their fingers and whisper read. Provide descriptive, positive feedback.
[Blake], you read with wonderful expression!

Unit 3 Fluency Passage

Name _____

Fluency Passage

My goal is to read with 0–2 errors and ____ words correct per minute.

I read with ____ errors and ____ words correct per minute.

The Talking Drum

One day last year, Mr. Chapman brought a cool drum to class. It was 14
made of wood. It looked like a log without all its insides. Animal skin 28
covered the ends of the drum. He said it was an African talking drum. 42
Mr. Chapman held the drum under his arm and squeezed the strings 54
that held the skins. The drum made a deep dark sound. Mr. Chapman 67
squeezed the strings tight and hit the drum again. This time it made a 81
high sharp sound. Then Mr. Chapman played lots more sounds on the 93
drum. It was almost like the drum could talk! 102
"In Africa, these drums are part of music and stories," Mr. Chapman 114
said. "People also talk to others far away with these drums." 125

Homework
I've listened to my child read this passage twice. Date _____ Signed _____

20

3. Partner Reading: Repeated Reading (Checkout Opportunity)

While students are doing Partner Reading, listen to individuals read the passage. Work on accuracy and fluency, as needed.

4. Homework: Repeated Reading

Have students read the story at home.

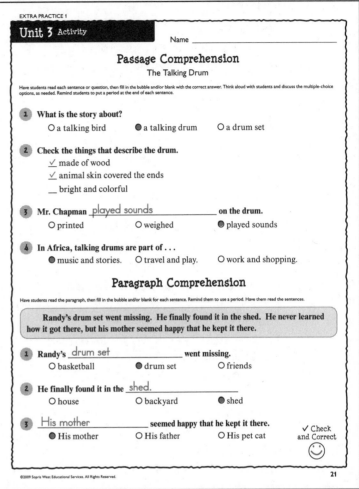

EXTRA PRACTICE 1

Unit 3 Activity

Name _____

Passage Comprehension
The Talking Drum

Have students read each sentence or question, then fill in the bubble and/or blank with the correct answer. Think aloud with students and discuss the multiple-choice options, as needed. Remind students to put a period at the end of each sentence.

1. **What is the story about?**
   ○ a talking bird　　● a talking drum　　○ a drum set

2. **Check the things that describe the drum.**
   ✓ made of wood
   ✓ animal skin covered the ends
   ___ bright and colorful

3. **Mr. Chapman** _played sounds_ **on the drum.**
   ○ printed　　○ weighed　　● played sounds

4. **In Africa, talking drums are part of . . .**
   ● music and stories.　　○ travel and play.　　○ work and shopping.

Paragraph Comprehension

Have students read the paragraph, then fill in the bubble and/or blank for each sentence. Remind them to use a period. Have them read the sentences.

> Randy's drum set went missing. He finally found it in the shed. He never learned how it got there, but his mother seemed happy that he kept it there.

1. **Randy's** _drum set_ **went missing.**
   ○ basketball　　● drum set　　○ friends

2. **He finally found it in the** _shed._
   ○ house　　○ backyard　　● shed

3. _His mother_ **seemed happy that he kept it there.**
   ● His mother　　○ His father　　○ His pet cat

   ✓ Check and Correct

©2009 Sopris West Educational Services. All Rights Reserved.　　21

Rhyming Words

High-Frequency Rhyming Words: new, few, grew, true, blue, saw, law, draw, rock, block

new	few	grew	chew	outgrew
true	blue	clue	glue	avenue
saw	law	draw	straw	seesaw
rock	block	shock	clock	windsock
junk	chunk	sunk	trunk	chipmunk

Related Words

protect	protected	unprotected	protecting	protection
care	careful	caring	uncaring	careless
bright	brighter	brightest	brightness	brightly
arrive	arrived	arriving	arrival	arrives
thank	thanked	thanking	thankful	thankless

High-Frequency Tricky Words

do	their	other	many	these
many	other	their	these	do
other	many	these	do	their
these	do	many	their	other
their	these	do	other	many

Available on CD-ROM

PROCEDURES

For each step, demonstrate and guide practice, as needed. Then have students complete the page independently.

1. Activity
Passage Comprehension
- Have students read each sentence or phrase, then fill in the bubble and/or blank with the correct answer.
- Think aloud with students and discuss the multiple-choice options, as needed.
- Remind students to put a period at the end of sentences.

Paragraph Comprehension
- Have students read the paragraph.
- Have students read each numbered sentence or phrase, then fill in the bubble and/or blank. Remind them to end sentences with a period, where needed.
- Have students read the completed sentences.

Self-monitoring
Have students read and check their work, then draw a happy face in the Check and Correct circle.

2. Word Fluency (BLMs are located on the CD.)
- To build fluency, have students read Rhyming Words, Related Words, and High-Frequency Tricky Words. Have students read each section three times in a row.
- To build accuracy, have students read all sets with partners.

ACCURACY BEFORE FLUENCY (Reminder)

Word Fluency is designed to build accuracy and fluency. Students should practice for accuracy before working on fluency.

PROCEDURES

1. Sound Review

Use selected Sound Cards from Units 1–3.

- Have students say each sound, building accuracy first, then fluency.
- Mix group and individual turns, independent of your voice.

2. Sounding Out Smoothly

- For each word, have students say the underlined part, sound out the word smoothly, then read the whole word. (Use the words in sentences, as needed.)
- Have students read all the words in the row, building accuracy first, then fluency.
- Repeat practice. Mix group and individual turns, independent of your voice.

3. Accuracy and Fluency Building

- For each task, have students say any underlined part, then read each word.
- Set a pace. Then have students read the whole words in each task and column.
- Provide repeated practice, building accuracy first, then fluency.

4. Tricky Words

Have students read each row for accuracy, then fluency.

5. Multisyllabic Words

For each word, have students read each syllable out loud, finger count the syllables, then tell how many syllables are in the word. If needed, use the word in a sentence. Have students read the whole word.

6. Dictation

green, grin, grand, back, black, crack

- Say "green." Have students say the word. Guide students as they finger count and say the sounds. Have students touch or write the sounds, then read the word.

  The first word is **green.** Say the word. (green)

  Say and count the sounds in **green** with me.

  Hold up one finger for each sound. /g/•/rrr/•/ēēē/•/nnn/ How many sounds? (four)

  What's the first sound? (/g/) Touch under /g/.

  What's the next sound? (/rrr/) Touch under /rrr/.

  What's the next sound? (/ēēē/) Write /ēēē/ with the e-e pattern.

  What's the last sound? (/nnn/) Touch under /nnn/.

  Read the word. (green)

- Repeat with "grin" and "grand."
- Continue with the rhyming words: back, black, crack.

Unit 3 Decoding Practice

Name _____

1. SOUND REVIEW Use selected Sound Cards from Units 1–3.

2. SOUNDING OUT SMOOTHLY Have students say the underlined part, sound out and read each word, then read the row.

s<u>ou</u>th	sk<u>y</u>	st<u>ar</u>s	n<u>igh</u>t

3. ACCURACY/FLUENCY BUILDING Have students say any underlined part, then read each word. Next, have students read the column.

A1 Sound Practice	**B1** Word Endings	**C1** Rhyming Words	**D1** Buildups
f<u>l</u>ew	<u>land</u>ed	<u>look</u>ed	c<u>are</u>
<u>n</u>ew	<u>help</u>ed	<u>cook</u>ed	c<u>are</u>ful
	<u>miss</u>ed		c<u>are</u>fully
slept		<u>told</u>	
t<u>en</u>ts	**B2** Reading by Analogy	<u>fold</u>	color
	<u>o</u>pen		colorful
eas<u>y</u>	<u>o</u>ver	**C2** Bossy <u>E</u>	
happ<u>y</u>	<u>o</u>nly	n<u>o</u>ses	danger
	hipp<u>o</u>	sc<u>a</u>re	dangerous
	pr<u>o</u>tect	l<u>i</u>fe	
		f<u>i</u>re	

4. TRICKY WORDS Have students read each row for accuracy, then fluency.

Ⓐ	because	monkey	people	eyes	their	5
Ⓑ	world	often	were	who	wasn't	10

5. MULTISYLLABIC WORDS Have students read the word by parts, tell how many syllables are in the word, then read the whole word.

Ⓐ	Mol•ly	Molly	riv•er	river
Ⓑ	sis•ter	sister	din•ner	dinner
Ⓒ	ad•ven•ture	adventure	Af•ri•ca	Africa

6. DICTATION Say the word. Have students say the word, then finger count and say the sounds. Have students say each sound as they touch or write it.

A1 Vowels	**B1** Rhyming Words
g r <u>ee</u> n	b <u>a</u> <u>c</u> <u>k</u>
g r <u>i</u> n	b l <u>a</u> <u>c</u> <u>k</u>
g r <u>a</u> n d	c r <u>a</u> <u>c</u> <u>k</u>

22

PROCEDURES

1. First Reading

Mix group and individual turns, independent of your voice. Have students work toward an accuracy goal of 0–2 errors and practice any difficult words.

2. Second Reading, Timed Reading: Repeated Reading

- Once the group accuracy goal has been achieved, time individual students for 30 or 60 seconds while the other children track with their fingers and whisper read.
- Determine words correct per minute. Record student scores. Celebrate when students reach their goals!

  Wow! [Nicole], you met your goal. That was your best score ever. You get to read into the recorder this week.

3. Partner Reading: Repeated Reading (Checkout Opportunity)

While students do Partner Reading, listen to individuals read the passage.

Work on accuracy and fluency, as needed.

4. Homework: Repeated Reading

Have students read the story at home.

Word Fluency B worksheet

EXTRA PRACTICE

Unit 3 Word Fluency B

Name _____

Rhyming Words

High-Frequency Rhyming Words: map, best, west, rest, more, score, store, before, bed, led

June	tune	dune	prune	Neptune
map	cap	strap	tap	catnap
best	west	rest	chest	southwest
more	score	store	chore	before
wed	sled	bed	led	dogsled

Related Words

travel	travels	traveled	traveling	traveler
ever	never	whenever	whatever	wherever
respect	respected	respectful	respectfully	disrespect
sleep	sleeps	sleeping	sleeper	sleepy
slip	slips	slipped	slipping	slippery

High-Frequency Tricky Words

some	would	into	has	two
two	some	has	would	into
has	into	two	some	would
would	two	some	into	has
into	has	would	two	some

©2009 Sopris West Educational Services. All Rights Reserved.

Activity worksheet

EXTRA PRACTICE 2

Unit 3 Activity

Name _____

Passage Comprehension
Wildlife Adventure

Have students read each sentence or question, then fill in the bubble and/or blank with the correct answer. Think aloud with students and discuss the multiple-choice options, as needed. Remind students to put a period at the end of each sentence.

1 Who is the main character?
- ● Molly
- ○ a team of people
- ○ wildlife

2 The new park was built to protect . . .
- ○ children.
- ● wildlife.
- ○ the tents.

3 Molly's job was to _count the hippos._
- ● count the hippos
- ○ tell stories
- ○ drive the jeep

4 Check the things that Molly and her team did at night.
- __ played drums
- ✓ cooked dinner over a fire
- ✓ told stories

Paragraph Comprehension

Have students read the paragraph, then fill in the bubble and/or blank for each sentence. Remind them to use a period. Have them read the sentences.

A baby hippo got stuck in the mud. The wildlife team pulled and pulled, but nothing happened. Then it rained, and the hippo slipped right out.

1 A _baby hippo_ got stuck in the mud.
- ○ mother hippo
- ● baby hippo
- ○ scientist

2 The wildlife team pulled and pulled, but _nothing happened._
- ○ the baby cried
- ○ the mud stuck
- ● nothing happened

3 Then it _rained_, and the hippo slipped right out.
- ● rained
- ○ splashed
- ○ hailed

✓ Check and Correct

©2009 Sopris West Educational Services. All Rights Reserved. 24

PROCEDURES

For each step, demonstrate and guide practice, as needed. Then have students complete the page independently.

1. Activity
Passage Comprehension
- Have students read each sentence or phrase, then fill in the bubble and/or blank with the correct answer.
- Think aloud with students and discuss the multiple-choice options, as needed.
- Remind students to put a period at the end of sentences.

Paragraph Comprehension
- Have students read the paragraph.
- Have students read each numbered sentence or phrase, then fill in the bubble and/or blank. Remind them to end sentences with a period, where needed.
- Have students read the completed sentences.

Self-monitoring
Have students read and check their work, then draw a happy face in the Check and Correct circle.

2. Word Fluency (BLMs are located on the CD.)
- To build fluency, have students read Rhyming Words, Related Words, and High-Frequency Tricky Words. Have students read each section three times in a row.
- To build accuracy, have students read all sets with partners.

> **ACCURACY BEFORE FLUENCY (Reminder)**
> Word Fluency is designed to build accuracy and fluency. Students should practice for accuracy before working on fluency.

PROCEDURES

1. **Sound Review**

   Use selected Sound Cards from Units 1–3.
   - Have students say each sound, building accuracy first, then fluency.
   - Mix group and individual turns, independent of your voice.

2. **Sounding Out Smoothly**
   - For each word, have students say the underlined part, sound out the word smoothly, then read the whole word. (Use the words in sentences, as needed.)
   - Have students read all the words in the row, building accuracy first, then fluency.
   - Repeat practice. Mix group and individual turns, independent of your voice.

3. **Accuracy and Fluency Building**
   - For each task, have students say any underlined part, then read each word.
   - Set a pace. Then have students read the whole words in each task and column.
   - Provide repeated practice, building accuracy first, then fluency.

4. **Tricky Words**

   Have students read each row for accuracy, then fluency.

5. **Multisyllabic Words**

   For each word, have students read each syllable out loud, finger count the syllables, then tell how many syllables are in the word. If needed, use the word in a sentence. Have students read the whole word.

6. **Dictation**

   red, read, bead, came, name, game
   - Say "red." Have students say the word. Guide students as they finger count and say the sounds. Have students touch or write the sounds, then read the word. Say something like:
   The first word is **red.** Say the word. (red)
   Say and count the sounds in **red** with me.

   Hold up one finger for each sound. /rrr/•/ĕĕĕ/•/d/ How many sounds? (three)

   What's the first sound? (/rrr/) Touch under /rrr/.
   What's the next sound? (/ĕĕĕ/) Write /ĕĕĕ/.
   What's the last sound? (/d/) Touch under /d/.
   Read the word. (red)

   - Repeat with "read" and "bead."
   - Continue with the rhyming words: came, name, game.

EXTRA PRACTICE 3

Unit 3 Decoding Practice

Name _____

1. SOUND REVIEW Use selected Sound Cards from Units 1–3.

2. SOUNDING OUT SMOOTHLY Have students say the underlined part, sound out and read each word, then read the row.

t<u>ai</u>ls	N<u>or</u>th	b<u>ir</u>ds	ch<u>ai</u>n

3. ACCURACY/FLUENCY BUILDING Have students say any underlined part, then read each word. Next, have students read the column.

A1 Sound Practice	**B1** Word Endings	**C1** Rhyming Words	**D1** Mixed Practice
gr<u>ew</u>	pick<u>ed</u>	b<u>ank</u>	l<u>ea</u>ves
n<u>ew</u>	read<u>ing</u>	th<u>ank</u>	<u>a</u>bout
s<u>aw</u>	go<u>ing</u>	dr<u>ank</u>	<u>a</u>lmost
<u>aw</u>esome	**B2** Bossy E	**C2** Compound Words	**D2** Tricky Words With Endings
th<u>i</u>ng	m<u>a</u>de	bookstore	want<u>ed</u>
th<u>i</u>nk	h<u>o</u>me	another	learn<u>ed</u>
trip	t<u>i</u>me	earthquakes	fac<u>ed</u>
	c<u>u</u>te		

4. TRICKY WORDS Have students read each row for accuracy, then fluency.

| Ⓐ | many | island | cover | country | were | 5 |
| Ⓑ | beautiful | four | monkey | would | they | 10 |

5. MULTISYLLABIC WORDS Have students read the word by parts, tell how many syllables are in the word, then read the whole word.

Ⓐ	thou•sand	thousand	moun•tain	mountain
Ⓑ	Ja•pan	Japan	real•ly	really
Ⓒ	in•ter•est•ing	interesting	vol•ca•noes	volcanoes

6. DICTATION Say the word. Have students say the word, then finger count and say the sounds. Have students say each sound as they touch or write it.

A1 Shifty Words	**B1** Rhyming Words
r <u>e</u> d	c <u>a m e</u>
r <u>e a</u> d	n <u>a m e</u>
<u>b</u> ea d	g <u>a m e</u>

25

PROCEDURES

1. First Reading

Mix group and individual turns, independent of your voice. Have students work toward an accuracy goal of 0–2 errors and practice any difficult words.

2. Second Reading, Short Passage Practice: Developing Prosody

- Demonstrate how to read a line or two with expression. Read at a rate slightly faster than the students' rate. Say something like: Listen as I read the first two sentences with expression and phrasing. I'm going to emphasize certain words and pause between sentences.

  "Miss Tam was thinking about a new adventure. She thought her next trip might be to Japan."

- Guide practice with your voice. Now read the paragraph with me.

- Provide individual turns while others track with their fingers and whisper read. Provide descriptive, positive feedback. [Camilla], you read with wonderful expression!

EXTRA PRACTICE 3

Unit 3 Fluency Passage

Name _____

Fluency Passage

My goal is to read with 0–2 errors and ____ words correct per minute.

I read with ____ errors and ____ words correct per minute.

Reading Adventure

Miss Tam was thinking about a new adventure. She thought her next trip might be to Japan. So Miss Tam went to the bookstore and picked out a book that was all about Japan. — 11 / 25 / 34

First she read that Japan is a chain of islands. Most people in Japan live on one of four big islands. Miss Tam learned that mountains cover the islands, and many of the mountains are volcanoes. The volcanoes set off more than one thousand little earthquakes a year! — 48 / 61 / 72 / 82

Miss Tam also wanted to learn about the animals in Japan. She found a book about red-faced monkeys that live in Japan. She really wanted to see the monkeys! — 94 / 107 / 112

Miss Tam found many more interesting books to read. Reading about Japan was almost as fun as going there. — 122 / 131

Homework
I've listened to my child read this passage twice.   Date _____   Signed _____

©2009 Sopris West Educational Services. All Rights Reserved.   26

3. Partner Reading: Repeated Reading (Checkout Opportunity)

 While students do Partner Reading, listen to individuals read the passage. Work on accuracy and fluency, as needed.

4. Homework: Repeated Reading

 Have students read the story at home.

PROCEDURES

For each step, demonstrate and guide practice, as needed. Then have students complete the page independently.

1. Activity

Passage Comprehension

- Have students read each sentence or phrase, then fill in the bubble and/or blank with the correct answer.
- Think aloud with students and discuss the multiple-choice options, as needed.

Paragraph Comprehension

- Have students read the paragraph.
- Have students read each numbered sentence or phrase, then fill in the bubble and/or blank. Remind them to end sentences with a period, where needed.
- Have students read the completed sentences.

Self-monitoring

Have students read and check their work, then draw a happy face in the Check and Correct circle.

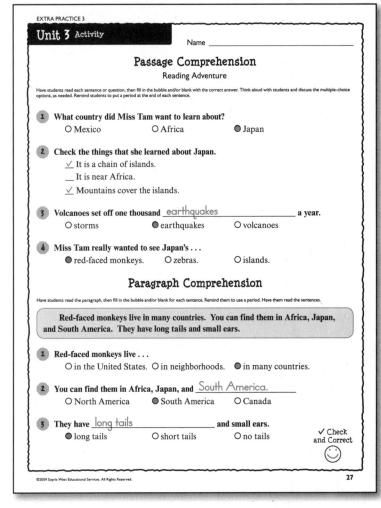

2. Word Fluency (BLMs are located on the CD.)

You may wish to have students practice with Unit 3 Extra Practice, Word Fluency A or B.